CHAMELEONS

CHAMELEONS

▼

Where Has The Honor Gone

Arthur E. Gerringer

Authors Choice Press

San Jose New York Lincoln Shanghai

Chameleons
Where Has The Honor Gone

Authors Choice Press
an imprint of iUniverse.com, Inc.

For information address:
iUniverse.com, Inc.
5220 S 16th, Ste. 200
Lincoln, NE 68512
www.iuniverse.com

ISBN: 0-595-20146-6

Printed in the United States of America

DEDICATION

Someone once said, and I do not recall whom it was, that behind every great man stands a great woman. Well, I cannot say that I am a great man, even though I have tried to be the best I know how. Yet, I can say that standing behind me is a great woman, the love of my life, Betty or Babe, as I call her. My wife has stood beside me, with me and sometimes even in front of me, through the nettlesome thick and the ruinous thin. She has followed me from post to post, problem to problem and triumph to triumph. In no small measure is my past success due to her loyal and loving support. She listened to me rail in the face adversity and she supported those decisions that seemed to destine her and me for the scrap heap. She has always been there and I know she always will be there. I could not have done my duty and written this meager work, without her.

I also want to pay homage to the one man in my life who, although simplistic himself, had a mind of such intricacy and determination that he could see what the future held and had, not only the duty and responsibility, but also the will and desire, to teach me right from wrong. My father, and also my mother, Elmer and Mary, set the stones of the foundation that has served me all of these years. I recall my father telling me, doing right is not hard, it is knowing when you are right that is hard. I wish mom could be here to read this, as she so anxiously awaited the reading of my previous efforts.

Further, I cannot forget to mention two people who mean more to me than life itself. My daughter, Rachel Dawn, lovingly referred to as Monkey and my red headed son, Douglas Kris, known throughout the world only as Kip. Kip and Monkey have watched their old man do many a thing over the last thirty some years, some of which I know they did not agree with. No slam at the younger generation, but they could not always grasp the "why" of what I said or what I did. Yet, knock on wood, I am blessed to have the two greatest kids that God could ever bestow on any man. My son is a career NCO in Intelligence with the U.S. Army. He stands on that proverbial wall, in some most uncomfortable places around the world, and watches over our nation and his family. Monkey, well, she is a sterling example of the medical profession, an RN, who applies her skills in the saving of life and limb. Of course, as they got older, they also came to see that Dad wasn't the old idiot they had thought about from time to time and it is with their love and support and my hope for their future, that helped bring this small, but important, rendering of life to life.

Finally, I would like to dedicate this work to all of those men and women who proudly wear the badge. Those individuals, who resist all of the temptations and bear up under all of the pressures. That gallant sub-culture who says no to corruption and no to those within our ranks who would drag them down in to the abyss. They are the steady and unflinching group whose stand against the anti-society elements from without, only pales in comparison to their stand against those same perpetrators from within.

Arthur E. Gerringer

INTRODUCTION

For just over thirty years, at the time this book was commenced, the author had served in the law enforcement profession, on the Federal, State and local levels. During those increasingly frustrating years it was repeatedly observed that the "profession" was not at the pinnacle that most behind a badge would like the sheep of society to believe. Now that is not to say that most of the men and women serving in the ranks of all types and sizes of agencies were not honest and ethical. It was not to say that most did not practice the highest principles and degrees of integrity. Rather, the opposite was true. Yet, the numbers within the "profession" that bring disrepute and disgrace upon themselves and their fellow law enforcement officers is growing and thus, in an at least equal proportion, the respect for the law enforcement profession is sinking.

There has been, and probably always will be, corruption within the ranks of law enforcement. That is a prophetic and unfortunately true statement, but it does not mean that influences cannot be brought to bear to reduce, and even possibly eliminate, such corruptive conditions. The seeds for this book have been observed on all too regular of a basis during the preceding thirty years, but the water to make the work blossom did not reach sufficient levels until 1996 and 1997. This book is written not to denegrate the entire profession, but rather to bring in to more concentrated view what this author and life long practitioner believes are the problems and how reality too often infects what should otherwise be a truly honorable profession.

Finally, the author wants to make it abundantly clear that this work is not written to satisfy the often ridiculous strictures of publishing adhered to by academics. Nor the convoluted standards of the raft of media types who see themselves as the only true writers of truth. This work is penned from the memory of an aging officer of vast experience and tumult. It is based on personal experience, even with a tint of prejudice, not racially motivated, but prompted by incompetence, corruption, inefficiency and stupidity of many whom should have been and known better. In the 1950's a hit television program began entitled Dragnet. Sergeant Joe Friday became famous for the utterance of the line, "Just the facts ma'am" and at the beginning of each show there would be the disclaimer that only the names had been changed to protect the innocent. Well, I am not as famous as Joe Friday and there will be no television show, but in this case, only the names have been changed to protect the guilty.

Corruption is not a solely outside, overpowering and degenerative influence. Quite the opposite, corruption is a mindset, an internal weakness, a lacking of character, a void of ethics, a bankruptcy of integrity, that can be laid at the feet of the individual who allows him or herself to become involved in such compromising activities. The outside influence only provides the momentary excuse or cause of action…

The Author

CONTENTS

Corruption comes in many forms.

The Author

CHAPTER ONE

THE INITIATION

It is August of 1997. There are only three ways out of the Lower Rio Grande Valley of Texas. One is up and along the Rio Grande River towards and through the City of Laredo. Another runs north from McAllen, Texas towards San Antonio and the third is north from Brownsville, along the eastern edge of the State towards Corpus Christi and points east and north.

No matter which route you take or how many back country and desolate country roads you may drive, you have to pass through permanently established U.S. Border Patrol checkpoints. These static and secondary points allow the Border Patrol agents to try and interdict the flow of illegal aliens and narcotics in to the interior of the United States. It is a tough and thankless job, fraught with danger and boredom.

On this particularly hot, dry and wind driven day I was driving my increasingly delapidated 1978 Chevrolet pickup north up the highway between McAllen and San Antonio. The pickup was loaded with those few possession and items of furniture that I had kept to live with while serving as the Chief of Police for the City of Donna, Texas. Traveling north from McAllen you become mesmerized by the vastness of the land and its barren nature. The countryside which extends from the blacktop presents little more than cactus, mesquite brush and rattlesnakes to look at. It is populated by the sparsely present rancher, Mexican illegal aliens trying to sneak north and the ever present drug smugglers. It is a forbidding territory with little or no redeeming values. Baked by the sun and continually thirsting for rain, it is a tough land and generally unforgiving to the novice.

About fifty miles north of McAllen the traveler comes upon numerous warning signs in English and Spanish that they are approaching a U.S. Border Patrol check point. Upon getting closer you observe that the roadway has been widened and directed to a couple of inline mobile home type buildings connected to a large covered parking area with marked driving lanes. From this portal to greater economic and individual freedom, green uniform clad men and women intently watch the approaching traffic, check license plates in the computer and question drivers and passengers as to their citizenship, destination and other questions which may shed light on the persons encountered. This is a chokepoint for drug traffickers and alien smugglers. The Falfurrias check point, is a wide spot in the highway, which attempts to serve as a barrier to criminality.

I pulled in to the first lane and stopped at the designated position and greeted the young hispanic Border Patrol agent. The expected questions as to my citizenship and destination were asked, and answered. The officer waved me on and I told him to be careful and good luck. As I drove out of the checkpoint I reflected on the some what futile nature of the duty, as well as the recently transpired events which led to my journey. In fact, I began to remember and even re-live, the preceeding twenty-seven years of "serving the public" and my country. Driving with road hypnosis I reviewed the past year first. Trying to unscramble the vagueries of what and why. I continued on until I came to the State of Texas, Department of Highways and Public Transportation built convenience or road side park.

In fact, it was located in between the north and southbound lanes of the blistering blacktop. I pulled in to stop and stretch my legs and to relieve a bulging bladder. Standing under a scraggly and twisted pin oak tree for shade, I watched a small four inch long lizard known as a Chameleon skitter across the hot asphalt to a point in the scrub grass that would be cooler for his undoubtedly overly warm feet. Observing this castoff of the dinosaur era, I saw something, not for the first time, but for the first time I had paid any real attention to it, that warranted more watching.

As this pint sized lizard crawled across the blackened surface of the pavement, its skin was a closely pigmented color. It was his disguise, a protective colorization to provide a higher degree of personal security from natural predators. Upon entering the short and stubby weeds, sparsely interspersed with what passes for grass, the surface of the lizard's back began to change color. In just a relatively short period of time the lizard had changed the color of his skin to closely match that of the newly arrived upon surroundings. A fact of nature, undoubtedly acquired over the years of mutation, lends safety to the meager life of the Chameleon. At various points, in the grass and on the pin oak tree, the Chameleon became almost indiscernible to the naked eye. Hard to see, even almost invisible, to all but the most determined of viewers. It was ironic, but this member of the lower cast of characters populating the surface of the world, gave a small, but essential clue to a much larger, people oriented problem.

I got back in my labored and cooled off pickup and began to pull out of the designated parking area, and upon starting to drive away, I glanced back at the spot where the Chameleon had been resting. I instinctively knew that he was still there, but I could not see him. He was laying there in wait for a juicy morsel of sustenance in the form of an ant or a fly or other creature upon which he sustains his existence. At that moment, many memories came flooding back as I continued on toward my wife and hopefully a more sane environment and secure occupational future.

Yet, I could not then, and even until now, get the image of that lowly lizard out of my mind.

Six months earlier I had loaded up most of our furniture, clothing, household items and other belongings, along with my wife, and moved her to safer surroundings in San Antonio. The first six months of my tenure as Chief of Police in the City of Donna had been somewhat harrowing for me, even a royal pain in the ass, but for my wife it had been the worst circumstances she had experienced since our marriage in 1973. She was scared, and not just for herself either. We had previously lived in tough places and through my employment, we had experienced some tough situations and individuals, but this was the worst to date. Why scared? Well, three death threats over the telephone, a continuous barrage of very ugly, coarse and verbally abusive telephone calls at all hours of the day and night. My wife was followed on more than one occasion. Officers followed me on various occasions. A neighbor also interrupted two men attempting to tamper with my vehicle or to attach something to its under-carriage in the wee hours of the morning, and ran off when confronted. The past history of shootings, fire bombing of cars, the murder of inform-ants and the general resistance to anyone attempting to rid the city of cor-ruption, along with the current events, all added up to making life miserable and scary. The most obvious question then, is, why be there or once there, why stay? To answer that we have to go back in time, over thirty years of time, and look at how we got there and what laid the foun-dation for getting there. A long and twisting trail, dotted with family, Vietnam, school, Federal service, State service and much more. To under-stand the now, I have to take you back through then, for in all things of importance, the present is definitely connected to the past. Corruption is not a malady of humankind that suddenly surfaces over night. It is can-cerous in nature and by its very nature is a slowly creeping disease of weak-ness within the individual so afflicted. At the same time, no one wakes up one morning and finds themselves possessed of any particular mindset, temperance or ideology. These too are built over time and influences come from many sectors, activities and individuals.

My father is a kind, but tough, man with a steel trapped mind and unwavering attitude towards doing right. Growing up in his family was comfortable, hard at times, but uncluttered by ambiguity and indecision. My father is an accountant. He can work numbers and taxes with the ease of a duck in water. From my years in high school, my dad wanted me to go to college and become an accountant. His goal was for us to open a father and son business. A very laudable goal, not just for him either, but it was not the way I desired to go. In high school I began to look seriously at entering the law enforcement profession. Granted, there were problems within the law enforcement community in the nineteen sixties, but they were not drummed in the same expose nature that they are in recent years and decades. Police were men mostly, and some women, that were widely respected by the citizens of our country. They performed duties that were dangerous at times, but for the most part they did much to protect citizens. Now, in today's more liberal veins of thinking, there are no telling how many pundits and soothsayers who would argue that policing was bad then, but better now. Okay, lets give a little. There is no doubt that there was crime in the fifties and sixties. There is no doubt t hat there were citizens of that era that did not trust the police – at all. There is no doubt that there was police corruption in many cities and agencies across the nation. Yet, the fear of crime in that time frame did not generally detract from the overall respect of police by citizens. I was young, obviously, and not very worldly, to say the least. Yet, I too respected the police. It was a profession in which, even though it sounds trite, I felt I could be of help to the community. Maybe even making a difference. Yes, we have heard that a trillion times over the years, but it was my honest perception of my potential.

Upon graduating from high school, as a not too sterling student, I got lucky and was admitted to the only college that I ever wanted to attend— Texas A&M University.

Having been the sole bread winner in the family for almost two years, while dad was laid up, I did not think that conditions could be much tougher on me. Was I wrong. Going to college, as a poor student, is hard enough, but then paying for it with no money, now that is hard. I worked and worked. Most of the time I had three jobs at a time, to make the money needed to pay the tuition and buy the books and to participate in all the Corps of Cadets had to offer and more. Needless to say, it was not easy. My grades, well, all I can say is, to this very day I owe a debt to my Dean, Charles McCandless. He knew my situation and how much I was working and did all he could to help me academically. In the end, I made it. I am proud to say, that my foundation of integrity and respect was laid at home through the guidance and upbringing from my parents. In addition, my years at Texas A&M University, has to receive a high five for my development. I take no shame in saying that it was those years that really prepared me to stand for right and do right. Texas A&M and the Corps made me a man. Although the overall program deserves the credit, there was one incident that served as a pivotal point. The original intent of the incident was not to provide an impetus to a positive result, but that was the ultimate outcome, much to the chagrin of those perpetrating the incident. In fact, in the short run, the outcome was not one desired by myself. Yet, the fire of the incident, hardened the steel of resolve and reinforced a life long mindset.

About 99.9% of law enforcement officers, even the feds, adhere to the unwritten code of silence. As we will see, that is wrong. The Corps of Cadets at Texas A&M University, then, and for decades preceding my attendance, was a military school. That is one of the reasons why I wanted to go there. The Corps was a tight knit group of young men. You did what you were told and you did not divulge what may go on that was not exactly, shall we say, kosher. As a Fish, or freshman, I was the lowest form of person on the campus, except for the non-regs or non-members of the Corps. There were more rules than you could shake a stick at, and you had to memorize them all. In a way, the regimen, the rules, the practices, the pranks, and the hazing were all intended to tear the individual down and then as time marched on, to rebuild and remold you into a more knowledgeable and more capable individual. Most of it was harmless, though mentally tasking. Yet, once in a while things got out of hand. I have not verbalized this story before, because it went against the grain of the "code" and while the result was right, maybe, just maybe the method was wrong.

On this particular night I returned from the library, trying to keep up with my studies, and upon arriving at my dorm room I took down my "pass" to be out of the room during study time. When I entered the militarily sparse room, I saw my roommate laying on the bunk bed clad only in a pair of blood soaked blue jeans. He was sobbing heavily. I ask what had happened and was told that my roomie had been caught out of the room by our sadistic sophomore. The punishment, by the sophomore, was to beat the bare butt of my roommate with a bent coat hanger. My roommate's posterior was badly cut and bruised. Much of the blood had tried and made the blue jeans stick to his tattered hide. I lifted him up and carried him to the shower just down the hall. Once there, I turned the water in the shower stall on and began to soak his jeans so that he could get them off. I also wanted him to go to the hospital to get treatment. He refused that idea as it would cause many questions, requiring answers, and that would generate more problems. Or at least he thought it would. Well, we got caught in the shower, out of the room, without permission. The same sophomore did not push it that night, but made it clear that both of us had to be at his room the next morning before formation. At the appointed hour, with no small degree of trepidation, we were there. Once ordered in to the room, we were berated verbally for the violations. Then, knowing what had caused the so called violations, the sophomore told us both to drop our pants. He reached under his mattress and retrieved a bent coat hanger. The hook had been taped to provide a better grip. We were to get our bare butts beaten. My roommate, did not want it. In fact he could not stand such an additional assault. He began to tear, but not knowing what else to do, he stepped out in to the center of the room. I thought to myself, this is absolutely crazy, not to mention wrong. My roommate could be permanently injured. The minor violation did not warrant such a brutal punishment. This was not right. In fact it was totally wrong. The sophomore approached me and ordered me to strip. Without thinking, I replied firmly, as we stared at each other, that if he was going to beat me, he better go get some more help. I found myself meaning exactly what I had said. For the response, I was slapped. He couldn't even hit me like a man, and from that day forward, there was no respect on my part for this bully. Yet, we were ordered to leave the room. No beating took place. My roommate later thanked me, as he hauled his belongings out the door and left the school. He could not handle the beating and should not of had to, but more importantly, he didn't have that internal strength that he needed to stand on his own. I am not putting him down. He was a damn nice guy and later graduated from Duke University. I missed him.

For the next many weeks, hell hath no fury like a pompous sophomore who has had his "authority" challenged. The word was quickly spread around the company that I was a problem. I was ostracized, not only by the upper classmen, but also by the individuals in my own class. Humiliation and physical exhaustion were the order of the day, the week, the month. You name it and they thought it up for me to do. The money I paid to the school, included three meals a day in the mess hall. I did not eat a meal in the mess hall for almost three months. The expense of having to eat at the Memorial Center or elsewhere was killing my budget and my parents could not understand the need for the extra cash. Upon returning to the dorm room one day I found all of my belongings packed and sitting outside the door. That was their call for me to leave campus. As the saying goes, even today, Highway 6 runs both ways.

Well, I had put up with everything they had thrown at me, and was damn near at my physical end, but this action really worked. Not to get me to leave campus, but to vow to stay on, come hell or high water. I stuck and toward the end of the year, much to my great surprise, several of the other freshmen came in to my room and offered me an apology. They stated that they now understood why I had stood up to the sophomore in the beginning. I cannot say that I was gushing with acceptance, but I knew then, and even more so later, that it took a lot for those guys to come in that way. After all that I had been through, it was of little solace on the one hand, but of immense importance on the other.

I am no hero or saving angel, but truth, honor, and duty were keystones of those years and I took them seriously. While a student at one of the greatest schools in the country, I got a job through the University that was to add impetus to my occupational goal. I became a dispatcher for the College Station and University Police Departments and the University Fire Department. This work gave me a keen insight in to the functioning of police and allowed me to learn directly from several of the officers that worked in those departments. Shortly after that I got on with the local Constable as a part-time Deputy and worked parties, dances and the like. It wasn't the most intense duty, to say the least, but it added to the education. After several years of tough rowing I received my degree. The next day I got my orders for the Army. This was to prove to be the next phase of my "education".

While at Texas A&M University, I tried to honor the wish of my dad, by majoring in Accounting, but it just wasn't to be. I changed my direction and went in to History and Political Science. Focusing on the Soviet Union. My immediate goal was to join the FBI or the CIA or some similar agency. Alas, it was not to be. It turned out that my peepers suffered from the defect of being partially color blind. That had kept me from flying for the Navy, and would keep me from joining the FBI. As for the CIA, well, they were polite, but said I had no asset that they were looking for. So, I packed my personal items and headed for the U.S. Army. Now in 1969, it did not take a genius to figure out where one would be ultimately going. I knew that Vietnam was on my travel itinerary. So, within a shorter amount of time than may have been desired, I found myself sitting in the middle of the Big Green War. The list of lessons learned from that sojourn is extensive. For the next year I walked enough miles to qualify for all the Mileage Plans that all the airlines together offer today. I don't mind saying that I was scared from the day I landed to the day I took off, but through it all, duty, honor and country kept me on track. No, that is not just a platitude, it was the only way to go. During my tour, I saw, heard and was intimately involved in a pack of very strange and damn dangerous situations. I came home with a chest full of medals and a deep respect for a tough job. Yet, for the all the funny, sad and tearful experiences, the one that I remember most had nothing to do with whistling bombs, zinging bullets, thirst, hunger, pain and the fear of death.

The chartered MAC flight that took a plane load of us to Long Binh was long and you could have cut the tension with a butter knife. After the aircraft landed and came to a stop on the tarmac, its load of FNG's started filing off. When I approached the door at the front of the cabin, a very attractive stewardess was standing there saying goodbye, and she was silently crying. She did not know me, or us, from Adams house cat, but she really cared. I have never forgotten that, for it was in startling contrast to the attitude of far too many people back in the "world".

Once in country I did a stint in the bush with the 9th Infantry Division, before the division was rotated back to the States. Then I was transferred to the 25th Infantry Division (Mechanized), which was also known as Tropical Lightning and the Wolfhounds. My rank increased and on two occasions I zigged when I should have zagged and, well, you can figure the rest. Then the 25th got to go home, so it was off to the 1st Cavalry Division (Airmobile). Having been wounded and with two letters of commendation from my previous commanding officer, I was selected to work as an Intelligence Analyst in the Tactical Operations Center. This work added to the cement for my years of work yet to come. Of course, having been successful in combat operations, I was "volunteered" to be a part of a seven man special operations team. Brother, that work would age a fella in a hurry. Well, eleven months and twenty-nine days after stepping off the "freedom bird" into the land of the "little people", I declined a direct field commission, hitched a ride on a Cobra to Long Binh, slept on the tarmac for a day and a half, and then boarded my ride back to the States. I had gained thirty pounds in weight, left my blood in a few spots of ground and had seen a lot of good men give their all. Being back in the "world" seemed strange in many ways, but for all the tumult and dissension, I kept my eyes on the horizon and knew where I was headed. Assigned to Ft. Sam Houston I began mailing out resumes and completing applications for Federal law enforcement positions. My active duty status was quickly coming to an end and with the stroke of a pen, I transferred to the Reserves and kept up my background in intelligence by going to the Army Security Agency. I went to several interviews and took several physicals, but in the end, I was offered employment with the United States Marshal Service. So I was going to be a Federal Agent and needless to say, I was really proud of myself. The refrain of duty, honor and country continued to ring in my head. My education was only just beginning and while I had been through quite a bit to date, my initiation in to the real world was far from complete. In fact, it was only the beginning. Two things were, or are now, for certain. My attitude was set in stone and that attitude would be mightily tested, time and again.

Principles and integrity are too often worn like velcro tabs on a uniform. They are put on and taken off at will, as the situation dictates.

The Author

CHAPTER TWO

THE OATH

Millions and millions of men and women have stood solemnly in thousands of rooms, facing Old Glory, all across the nation, with their right hand raised, and swore an oath of allegiance to the United States. That oath also committed its takers to defend the Constitution of the United States, against all enemies, foreign and domestic. These individuals took the oath, joining one of the military services of our nation, accepting the duties of an elected member of our government and upon being employed as a law enforcement officer.

In August of 1969 I stood in a small room in Dallas, Texas with about forty-five other young men and listened to a U.S. Army Captain recite the oath, which we repeated in unison. On that warm and sultry day I became a member of the United States Army, and proudly so. The Corps of Cadets had prepared me, at least in the intangible ways, and the Army would provide the hone to sharpen my skills and knowledge. The first stop was Ft. Bliss and then on to Ft. Ord, before making the big move to South Vietnam. Since I had been in college and then on to the service, I was a few years older than most of the men with whom I entered upon duty in the defense of my country. Leadership came easy, but it was the followship of those within my unit that took a lot of work to convince them to achieve. There were a few occasions where the intolerant attitudes of one or two caused situations that could have quickly worsened, but calm, introspection and persuasion succeeded in bringing order to a potentially violent situation. It was then and continues to be to this day an unfathomable puzzle as to why people strive so mightily to denegrate others in the name of power. What is even more sad and at times funny, is that many of those who engage in such ridiculous conduct have about as little "power" as can be imagined. So why do they bully, manipulate and intimidate? If anyone ever figures out the universal answer to that question, they can bottle it and make a lot of money.

My years on active duty were an eye opener. For the military and those who directed the military and supported the military, it was a damn tough time. I did then, and still do today, believed that the war in Vietnam was right. Needless to say there were many who did not, and probably still do not, believe that way. However, I believe that history will show, once we get past the pall that still hangs over the nation because of that war, that the effort to stop communism was right. What was wrong was the micromanagement that went on in the daily conduct of the war. There was a lacking of solid objective. There were too many daily inputs from political officials in decisionmaking processes about how to prosecute the war. What I can say in opposition is that many fine young men and women departed there earthly bounds, involuntarily, due to the lies, stupidity and unabashed incompetence of many who had a directing hand in the operations taking place in Vietnam. Where was their memories? How easily they forgot—duty, honor, country.

The attitude of many, mostly the enlisted personnel, who served in Vietnam was fueled by the sights and sounds generated by the anti-war people who were in the United States. Yet, for all the anti-war sentiments within the ranks, based upon political ideology, tactical disagreements, strategic disputes or influences, far too many men and women, frivolously and conveniently forgot the oath that they had taken. Granted, I did not like the way some things were being done or the way in which some were treated, but what many also conveniently forgot was that with rights and privileges came responsibilities. So we trudged along and the quagmire became thicker.

Now I would be, in my humble opinion, remiss in unleashing barbs if I did not include in the quiver some salient points concerning the members of the media who scurried about the streets of Saigon and other relatively safe places reporting on the horrors of the war. NO reporter, that I know of, takes an oath like those who served in the ranks. They may want everyone to believe that they are strict constitutionalists, believing in the sanctity of the First Amendment, but I do not believe that the majority of common sense thinking people really imbibe in that nectar of deceit. We have all heard that now familiar refrain, the people have the right to know. Okay, let us agree. We do have a right to know. The truth! Not the truth as shaped by personal beliefs, likes and dislikes. Not the truth as driven by the desire to become famous or infamous. Not the truth as staged by Jane Fonda and others of that ilk. Not the truth as shaped by the potential for truth as dictated by polls, ratings and political influences. As Joe Friday said on many occasions, "Just the facts". As a media person, staunchly believing in the First Amendment, reporters not only have a right to report, but they also have a responsibility to report the facts. It can be easily argued that they also take an oath, an unofficial oath, but an oath nevertheless, which is no less demanding in its expectancy of adherence. We could have a long and tedious "discussion" about which individuals who swear the oath are more susceptible to that oath or of whom more is expected once having taken the oath.

For example, who should be expected to adhere to their oath more religiously, the soldier who works in intelligence for the U.S. Army or, say, the President of the United States? The soldier, well, he has been in the service of his country for six years and has attained the rank of Sergeant. He is involved in the collection and analysis of highly sensitive information. His position and his functions of that position are classified TOP SECRET. The soldier voluntarily took on the duties and responsibilities of his position. The work the soldier performs is only a small percentage of the overall intelligence mission of all the services and agencies within the United States. The soldier is twenty-four years old and earns about $28,000 a year. The soldier is stationed in such glamorous environs as Turkey, South Korea, Ft. Huachuca or Bad Aibling. For the soldier, especially if he has a family, the strains will be difficult, and financially almost unbearable. If he or a member of his family needs medical attention, they will probably sit in a waiting room for hours, and under the latest policies will probably have to pay, out of pocket, for a greater share of the cost. The stresses and strains can be tremendous. The separations from family can be extensive. In fact, the soldier may even be on welfare and having to feed his family with food stamps. Yet, for all the trials and tribulations, the soldier is expected to show up at his post and to perform his duties in an exemplary manner. Any breach of his oath, civilian law or the Uniform Code of Military Justice, will put him, and his family, in jeopardy. If a serious breach or a felony violation, the soldier will be prosecuted, possibly imprisoned, will lose his security clearance and most likely, dishonorably discharged from the service. Any or all of these actions will hang like a yoke around his neck for the rest of his life.

Now, the President of the United States, also voluntarily enters in to the position he so coveted. Yet, unlike the soldier, he has an income of $200,000 per year, at least officially. The President lives in the people's house, a mansion almost beyond compare. There are no extended stints of service in dangerous and forbidding climes. His family can always be with him. The President and his family can eat anything and as much as they desire. There is no welfare and no food stamps. The President has the ability to access any and all information, no matter how sensitive. If he or any member of his family become ill, they have immediate access to any doctor or hospital they desire, most particularly Bethesda. Yes, there are long hours in that position. Yes, the strains and stresses can be regular and difficult. Yes, there is a lot of responsibility that goes with the position of the President of the United States.

Both individuals have very important duties and responsibilities. Both individuals carry a burden on their shoulders, voluntarily accepted, to serve the people and the government of the United States. BOTH individuals voluntarily submit to the SAME oath of office. BOTH swear to uphold the law and defend the Constitution. At the same time, BOTH are citizens of the United States and are subject to the laws of the United States. Yet, if the President of the United States violates the law, particularly a felony, as we have witnessed in recent years, what happens to him? Richard M. Nixon was forced to resign the office. William J. Clinton, ...nothing! So, which of the two men should be held more responsible? To which of the two men does the oath apply more? Which of the two men should be more strictly, rigidly or firmly dealt with? Does it matter what felony law was broken? Does it matter that the Sergeant committed the felony in search of money to better the existence of his family? Does it matter that the President committed the felony to cover up his immoral and even possibly illegal conduct, a conduct that in itself would have serious ramifications for anyone in the military or in private enterprise? Which of the two men was guilty of dishonoring their oath to the nation more seriously? Which of the two men caused the greatest harm and dishonor to his nation? Are we a nation of laws or a nation of men? So we come to the ultimate questions. Is the oath sworn, to be taken seriously and adhered to? Is it rational and logical to hold one more accountable to the oath sworn than another? Is it what one says in an oath, to whom the oath is spoken or circumstances of any particular moment obligated under the oath, that the oath and its taker achieve serious accountability?

Obviously, at least as the majority would be concerned, one position is more prominent than the other. One position entails a much higher profile, daily exposure and seemingly the apex of power. So, can it be convincingly argued that the individual who is in the more powerful is less vulnerable? Or, more realistically, is it the individual who is in the more influential position, that is less vulnerable?

In September of 1971, after receiving the offer of employment with the United States Marshal Service, I went out and purchased a few new suits, shirts and ties. My concept of professionalism included presenting oneself in the best possible appearance. U.S. Marshal Sam Roberts was in command of the Western District of Texas and the Chief Deputy was Jack Graves. Still young and less than worldly, I was determined to learn all that I could and to perform in a manner that would distinguish me from all others, in a positive fashion of course. On the second day of coming true of my long held dream, I was summoned to the office of the United States Magistrate in the old Federal building and Courthouse, across from the Alamo. In retrospect, the location of the building and those who were officed therein was somewhat prophetic and destined. The Honorable John Giles was the U.S. Magistrate for the San Antonio Division. Giles was a tall and aging man upon whom physical and medical infirmities had attached themselves in an irreversible mode.

Yet, Magistrate Giles was a man of keen mind and dry wit. Standing in front of the judicially robed Magistrate, I followed his directives. In front of a small group of fellow agents and court personnel, I raised my right hand and repeated the oath of office to which I had been appointed. Slow and in sections, I swore to uphold the laws of the United States and to defend the Constitution, so help me God. Pride sprung forth from my inner being in a well spring of triumph. For the next ten years I worked in places and did things for the agency and the government, and thus the people, that I previously did not even know existed. Needless to say, those years were an education. Granted, I learned many things about the law enforcement profession and its various workings, but the damnedest part came in the revelations that accompanied the individuals, attitudes, ethics (or the lack thereof), and even their personal actions.

Marshal Sam Roberts was a political type. That is about the only way, in that era, that you could be "nominated" by a U.S. Senator from your State, to be appointed by the President of the United States to the position. Sam, like so many others had some type of influence within his party. Now, that is not to say that he or any other such appointee was not a good man or deserving of the appointment. Yet, I will say that there has been a number of individuals appointed to the position of U.S. Marshal that did not know doodle about the position, the profession or even or management, much less leadership. Sam Roberts, originally from Austin, Texas was the man who ultimately said yea or nay on my appointment and for any failings he was still a nice man. Within a year or so it became obvious that at least some of the personnel in the district did not like Roberts. Even in the early stages of my employment I had apparently made it plain that I was not a game player and did not bend over to pick up the soap for anyone. So, when I came to the office one morning I was and was not somewhat surprised to learn that Roberts was gone. It seems that there were some alleged irregularities in travel vouchers that had been filed and thus in funds that had been paid as reimbursements. Or at least that is what I was told. The other part that was more interesting and to a degree, sickening, was the fact that men of the San Antonio office had clandestinely made entry in to the locked office, desk and files of Roberts to locate and duplicate the allegedly incriminating records. Now I will be the first to admit that if Roberts had engaged in illegal activity his removal was necessary. At the same time, I observed and overheard the individuals involved in the discovery of this information, making not only light of Roberts, but were congratulatory of themselves for having brought Roberts down. It smacked of getting rid of an individual they did not like and the alleged violations were only the vehicle. This was the first encounter I had experienced with individuals who would go to any lengths to affect the changes that they felt were appropriate and it gave rise to other questions. Most notably, who in the hell endowed them with the sole ability and knowledge to decide, for everyone, who was best suited to hold office and how that individual was to conduct him or herself? There was in these men, a perverted blending of self-righteousness, the law, retribution and "we gotcha" mentality, veiled by legality of purpose. If true, I could not condone the actions of Roberts, but I also could not hold much respect for the individuals in the "uncovering" of the information. To what future extent might they bend? Who might be there next "target" of inquiry? There was a procedural manner established within the agency for such matters, yet no one availed themselves of it. Arguments can be made for both sides in the question of whether all the individuals upheld their oaths.

Shortly after Sam Roberts joined the ranks of the used to be's, James F. Johnson was elevated to the position of U.S. Marshal and with the assignment of Bob Christman as his Chief Deputy the district began to dispel some of its less than complimentary baggage. Of course, there were lesser actors within the district that were or became engaged in what can be graciously described as less than professional conduct, but to note them all would require a highly photographic memory and a couple of volumes in which to record them. Suffice it to say, all was not as had been anticipated in the beginning.

For the next few years, until April of 1975, I performed a wide variety of duties. Some were great, some were good and some, while necessary, were the pits. Some of the more notable were the months spent at Wounded Knee during the takeover and violent conflict by Souix Indians of the Pine Ridge Reservation in South Dakota. The American Indian Movement (AIM) killed and or wounded a number of Federal Agents and were involved in acts of domestic terrorism around the country. There was the task force assignment in New York, which sought to bust up police corruption. There was the repatriation of Vietnamese citizens who had been spirited to the United States and then found that the streets were not paved with gold and they wanted to return to Vietnam. That was a babysitting job of immense expense and trouble for people whose gratitude for U.S. sacrifices on their behalf was motivated by even more selfish desires for more freebies. There was an assignment that would prove to be more memorable than many others. It is also another prime example of how men and women can so cavalierly ignore their oath and duties to country and God. I speak here of what even the most young among us know, or should know, as Watergate. Yes, Richard M. Nixon, former President of the United States, and his cronies, while occupying the most powerful office in the land, and probably the world, trampled on our laws, the flag and their oaths with single minded purpose. Let's see, the violators included, but were not limited to, the President of the United States, the Attorney General, Chief of Staff for the President, attorneys, former FBI agent and other politicians. Holding them all at Fort Holabird for months was revealing in the information that flowed and the ultimate feelings and interactions that ensued between men of power and that were friends. Was Nixon a great President, as many still argue? Very possibly! Nixon did do things for the country that were very noteworthy. However, Nixon also engaged in conduct that was clearly illegal, and I do not mean little or misdemeanor acts. Did Nixon receive the appropriate discipline for his long running illegal conduct? NO! Being forced from office was obviously a humiliating action, especially for an individual of immense ego. Yet, should Nixon have faced the bar of justice for felony violations, like any other citizen? Again, are we a nation of laws or a nation of men. Okay, President Ford pardoned Nixon and that action prohibited any criminal action against Nixon. That action to pardon was incumbent upon Ford for political reasons, but was it the right thing to do? Not the politically right thing to do. Well, we could argue over that for decades and not settle the question. In the last seven years we have once again been saddled with the criminal misconduct of a President and his followers and appointees. Only this time, the width and breadth of the problem has been even more extensive. President Clinton, his wife, personal attorneys, senior advisers, cabinet appointees, and many others have all been taken to task for their misdeeds. It is arguably the most corrupt administration to hit Washington, D.C. in the history of our young nation. Now, the question that is to be ask is, was the conduct of Nixon and his people, any more or less violative of the law than the conduct of Clinton and his crew? Absolutely not. What we saw with Nixon was a backlash of the people, at least partially motivated by the hatred of our involvement in Vietnam. Of course, the Democratic party, which has always seemed to have a better capability to punch hot buttons, did its part. At the same time, the mass of media, which is mostly viewed as being Democratic and liberal, also weighed in to influence the outcome, just as they did with the war in Vietnam. Now make no mistake, I do not condone the conduct of Nixon. In fact, there should have been a criminal prosecution. But, you can quickly become cynical about the system when you review what has taken place concerning Clinton. The media spin of what the President and his Democratic followers put out was mind boggling. Congress on the whole did not have the intestinal fortitude to do what was "right". The majority only played sematical games and ultimately what was politically right. Why? The main points given credit for this dismal state of affairs were the great state of the economy and that there has been a great change in the moral values of citizens.

Clinton, some would argue, has received his discipline in that he and his family have been greatly embarrassed and humiliated. That argument might hold more water if Clinton and his horde of accomplices had individual or a collective level of guilt, but from their displays during and since the revelations, it is obvious that they do not. The bottom line for them was winning the political battle. Right and wrong did not enter in to the equation. So they lied, destroyed or conveniently lost track of subpoenaed files, obstructed justice, suborned false testimony and even committed perjury. Not to mention a host of other acts by the Vice President and a whole phallanx of supporters. They took the same oath. They swore to uphold the laws and to defend the constitution. No where in the oath does it say, "when I want to or when it is convenient for me to do so or when it may not be supportive of what I perceive as what I have to do to remain in power". Where was all that honor for these leaders of the great experiment in democracy?

Sadly, in my humble opinion, the United States has been on a rocky and treacherous road of moral decay. I don't just mean abortion or drugs or any of the other umpteen subjects that get tossed around as motivating factors, but rather, I point to the fact that far too many citizens no longer have any respect for anything other than there own very narrow desires and goals. Along with the above motivators is the fact that our nation has become a hyphenated society, consumed with political subterfuge, official dis-information and over riding political correctness. We have become gluttonous and irresponsible.

On that sultry and bright September afternoon in 1971, U.S. Magistrate John Giles stepped down from his judicial bench and walked to the front in his long black robe of authority. Standing in front of me, frail and slightly unsteady on his feet, Judge Giles extended his right hand and grasp mine. His eyes were piercing and his handshake was like gripping a hot branding iron. As he shook my hand and congratulated me, he said a few simple words that were seared into my memory and were to have more impact than I then could fathom. To this very day, and probably until the day I draw my last breathe, I remember them vividly. His honor said, "Don't ever violate your oath". I quickly and without thinking replied that I would not. That reply was expected I suppose, and it is even possible that the Judge would not completely believe that I would hold true to my oath, but I can say with certainty and with a pride steeped in humility, that from that day to this, I have never violated my oath. Those simple words spoken on that milestone within my life were the cement of a bond that was greater than the words, stronger than the values they bound, and were to represent me in good stead for decades to come.

Trite? Maybe, to some. Surely, there will be those who will have an uproarious laugh at my knight in shining armor attitude, yet, my position is lucidly clear. Words are what men live by, or at least they should. Patriotism is not a dirty word or a shaggy raincoat to be donned momentarily to deflect refuse, but rather an old standard that has been borne by generations of good men and women.

EVIL FLOURISHES WHERE GOOD MEN DO NOTHING.

Unknown

CHAPTER THREE

LEADERSHIP

As this book is being penned, or rather computered, there exist a growing number of sullied actions, to say the least, on the part of law enforcement officers across the nation. Many of these men and women belong to more than one of the larger agencies in the country and have had long and sometimes checkered histories.

One such agency is the Los Angles Police Department. Another is the New York City Police Department. On the smaller end of the scale are agencies such as the Boerne Police Department and the Sheriff's Office of that rural, but growing part of Texas. Now there is plenty of troubling problems to go around and corruption is not limited to the "locals". Included in this mix of violative conduct are agents and other personnel of such paragons of virtue as the CIA, the FBI, the DEA, the INS, the branches of the U.S. Military and others. In fact, there is not an office, agency, organization or even a loose collective of personages that are not susceptible to or have been involved in corrupting situations.

If, which is not a question, corruptive conduct exists within all forms of entities, what is the common motivating factor(s)? Surely, due to resources, background investigations, individual compensation and benefits, education and numerous other established filtering systems, not all agencies have the proverbial rotten apple in their own barrels. If the reader agrees that it is unreasonable to believe, then the reader would be erroneous in such a belief. Whether it be the White House, the U.S. Congress, any Federal agency, including the FBI, a state agency, a county agency or a local agency, all have had their share. Fortunately or unfortunately, depending on your point of view or the position of the bureaucracy involved, some agencies and authorities are more adept at preventing their dirty laundry from being aired or at least at putting a control or spin upon the information to foster the most favorable impression.

Earlier, there was the question as to what were the motivating factors? Well, let us take a look at what are the "normally" provided or believed reasons that officials of government, including law enforcement personnel on all levels, become involved in corrupt misconduct. Since I am a member of the law enforcement community we will concentrate on that collection of people. The majority of the time, the reason given is that law enforcement personnel are paid a sufficiently high wage to provide them with the necessities for themselves and their families, and thus would permit them to avoid the "temptations" to becoming involved in corruption. Then there is the second alleged motivating factor, and that is sex. Well, we will not turn this work in to a lewd recounting of such activities, but that "need" has been a part of some incidents. We also have heard from the lips of violators that "I was afraid to NOT become involved because my partner or other officers were involved and I did not want to be on the outside or against them". So we call that peer pressure and fear. Then there is a motive that is as old as time itself. Revenge. Now this is a factor that is most commonly known to spur on men and or women who have undergone some relationship upheaval. Maybe the wife found out that her husband was cheating and set out to teach him a lesson. Or it could be an officer that received some kind of discipline from his superiors and decided to show them who was smarter. Then it could also be an individual who feels he was wrongly passed over for a promotion or was denied a raise for capricious reasons. Anyway, the reasons can be numerous and often confusing. Many times they defy logic and in the end not even the violator can clearly enunciate the reason. So, the individual sells information about an investigation or sensitive intelligence material or agrees to cause a course of action contrary to proper procedures or in a direction that will benefit a less than scrupulous soul. In most instances the money that changes hands is not all that great of a sum. Police officers are known to have engaged in criminal conduct for as little as $10.00. That is not enough to even pay for a tank of gasoline, much less to set up a far more comfortable retirement.

Now we come to the factor that gets far too many law enforcement personnel in hot water. Narcotics! Over the years I have worked some where in the neighborhood of about one thousand dope cases. Most were against the nickel and dime bag dealers that were or already had destroyed the quality of life in a small section of a community. There were a percentage of them that involved police officers, attorneys, businessmen, doctors, nurses, engineers, auto dealers, and even a judge. There were some that the amount of money involved and the drugs that were seized amounted to a pretty substantial sum. Then there was a handful, that the currency was staggering and the narcotics taken in to custody defied the imagination. The largest marijuana case amounted to over four tons. Talk about stinking, but the labor to move and store all of it was an undertaking in its own right. Finding an automobile trunk loaded with greenbacks is enough to stop your heart, but it happens all too frequently. For decades, far too long, the flow of narcotics in to this nation has been gargantuan. Tons and tons and tons of that damnable stuff has generated a multi-billion dollar "business" and the violence, death and destruction have associated with narcotics has kept pace with the increasing flow. Is the war on drugs having any success? Well, that would depend on your definition of success. Granted the quantity of narcotics seized by law enforcement has increased over the years. Even the amount of illicit money seized has increased. In fact the money seized is in the multi-tens of millions. So, if that is the measure of success, the war on drugs is a success. On the other hand, if you measure the degree of success in the terms of how much is "not" being seized and how much is being consumed and how many addicts there are, then the answer to the question is undoubt-edly—NO. Now no self-respecting dope trafficker, smuggler, producer or cartel kingpin is going to be bouyed by the fact that the drug police are tak-ing down large shipments of his "product", but then on the other side of the argument, is the fact that these intrepid souls expect to loose a certain amount. It is a built in business factor, a business loss, to be expected, planned for, anticipated and even regulated. Now how do you regulate a loss. Easy, you provide through layering of persons enough information that results in the police finding a load. That find will keep them happy, divert attention from other activities, tie up personnel and resources and is a price of doing business.

When I first joined the ranks of the U.S. Marshals, one of my first trips was to the United States Penitentiary at Leavenworth, Kansas. Had a cou-ple of rather difficult individuals who were designated to reside in that institution for a considerable number of years due to their less than ster-ling behavior within society. Arriving at the front parking lot and gate at about seven in the morning, it was a sight which left an impression. The morning was cool and lightly shrouded in a fog or mist. While waiting for the morning count to be completed, before being allowed entry to deposit our in custody refuse, I became enthralled with the immense and isolated nature of the edifice before me. The walls were at least twenty feet tall, constructed of concrete and topped with items that were not a compli-ment to exposed and escaping flesh. The steps up the main doors, if mem-ory serves me correctly, were thirteen, just like the number that led up to the hangman's noose on a gallows. I tried to imagine what it would take to cause me to commit an act, any act, that could lead to being confined to such a horrendous place for a long chunk of my life. I could not come up with even an imaginary act or fantasized dollar figure that could make such an existence worth the cost. Over the years, I have seized and or seen amounts of money that would stagger the imagination. Yet, I have never met or even heard of anyone that could produce a sum of money of such sufficiency to even tempt me to violate the law and land in prison. Now, like every other human being, I do not doubt that I have a price, but it is undoubtedly so damn high that I won't ever have to worry about anyone even thinking about trying to meet it.

Yet, almost everyday of the week, an officer, a clerk, a magistrate, an attorney, a banker, a laborer or any one of dozens of other walks of life—do. Now, dope, in its many forms, are intoxicating and destructive. Yet, there is another factor that influences individuals that in many ways is even more intoxicating and has the potential of being at least as destructive, if not more so, than narcotics. That much maligned endeavor, which has also existed since the beginning of organized human activity, is known as "Politics". Yep, there is no doubt about it, engaging in political activities has ruined many a man and woman, all in the name of serving our citizens. We only have to examine, even just lightly, the activites across the nation of the past two decades. In doing so we are hit right between the running lights with the fact that many political types engage in a whole host of activities that are illegal. Why? Well, again the reasons are as diverse as they are for any other type of profession, or no profession at all. Many acts are committed in an attempt to get in to the desired office or position and then, once there, other acts follow which are aimed at holding on to that office or position. It too, is a vicious circle, and the lame, lazy and honest, truly honest, need not apply. For to get in you have to have help. That help is going to cost, but what is the cost. A promise here, a job for a supporter or contributor there, turning your head on this issue, helping grease the wheels for a permit, or getting young Johnny out of a jam. On and on it goes and on and on flows the money and the influence. Someone once said that the only time you can trust a politician is when his or her mouth is shut, and even then it is a risk. From the local mayor or county commissioner to the President of the United States, I have never seen or heard one yet, that would not say whatever they thought was necessary, at the given moment, to influence and or persuade another or a group to do this or that. Once in office, it is katie bar the door when it comes to what is fair game to stay in office. Again, but on a much shorter time frame, we only need to look at what has transpired on the national scene to understand the length to what politicians will go to in order to maintain their acquired offices. Lies will abound, documents will be "lost", ridiculous amounts of time will be required to perform a subpoenaed task, witnesses will have their memories become missing, and conspiracies, both real and imagined, will abound. Over the thirty years of my working in law enforcement, on both the Federal, State and local levels, I have seen and heard "arrangements" that had varying degrees of influence upon the criminal justice system. In fact, politics, in all of its forms, has caused more obstruction of and destruction of quality law enforcement efforts than any other outside influence. All in the name of "politics" or "political survival", as it was perceived necessary at the moment.

A Chief of Police close to Lubbock changes the information on a citation to help a person of alleged influence out. A damn ticket of all things. It was discovered and it was illegal and adios to the Chief. A Sheriff west of San Antonio hires a buddy as a Chief Deputy, but the buddy does not have a law enforcement license and it is not only found out, but it too was illegal. A police union President in a major city, like San Antonio, takes bribes from attorneys, and it was found out and it too was illegal. A mayor coerces the Chief to tear up an investigative report and proposed charges for DWI to protect the son of a supporter. It was found out and was illegal. A U.S. Senator uses the power of his position to force a woman to engage in sexual conduct and that was illegal. A Federal law enforcement bureau director falsifies travel documents for money refunds or to utilize transport facilities for personal business and that is illegal. A police sergeant sells himself to a Mexican narcotics smuggler as a bodyguard for the smuggler, and that is illegal. A District Attorney blocks criminal investigations to prevent an ally from being taken to task for criminal conduct, and that is illegal. Needless to say, the list of examples goes on and on and on. The list is only limited by the imagination and peculiarities of the human mind. In fact, it gets pretty humorous at times, as the agencies that supposedly are allowed to investigate "lesser" agencies and personnel who violated the law, are themselves less than spic and span in their conduct. For political reasons, either in house or in the more formal political arena, survival is the name of their game. So, when the FBI lies about what it has or has not done, that blackens not only their collective eye, but also the eye of the rest of the profession, in the view of the citizens. Now, some of my friends and associates will quickly remind me that politics is involved in everything and you have to learn to play the game or you won't be allowed to play at all. That is true. Politics, an ugly scourge, has attached itself to damn near everything that we do, but I disagree that you have to play by "those" rules in order to continue to play or to be successful.

Now, we have given a glance at a lot of factors, which influence misconduct, but there is one overall influence that while it has been seen or obliquely touched on, has not been confronted head on. That factor is POWER. The root of many evils. Power is many things to different people. It may be a lot of money and the ability to buy and sell anything, including people. It may be the power of fear as produced by peers or instilled by the unknown factors of a vengeful act (s). It may be the lust for advancement to a position of more influence or import. It may be the type of power that can coerce individuals in to performing or not performing in a manner that they might not otherwise do. For far too many people, the possession of power is the essence of power and to relinquish power, voluntarily or otherwise, is perceived as a failure and not to be condoned or allowed. So, to maintain power, power is routinely perverted to the subjugation of others to that power. For the holder, the possession of power is all consuming and the use of power to enhance power knows no limits.

There is no argument, at least from this writer, and probably 99% of those who wear a badge, that the compensation received by a member of the law enforcement community is woefully shy of what it should be. But, I cannot agree with the often espoused notion that police officers go bad because of low pay. In fact, our nation is crawling with police officers that make dirt level wages and do not cross the line. So to what can we contribute their salvation from the sins of man? Self respect, a good upbringing, religious convictions, a true belief in the sanctity of the law, upstanding peers and influence, family support and other factors? The answer is yes to all, but there is one other item that we need to examine as a factor for both good or bad.

For more than twenty years I have been an instructor. I have taught law enforcement, military and civilian personnel at seminars, academies and colleges about a lot of topics, but one of my favorites has always been—Leadership.

Now leadership can be a force of good or it can be a force of bad. I am not talking about banging someone up beside the head with a piece of lumber labelled leadership. No, most often, it is a much more subtle influence. Take Sergeant Major of the Army Gene McKinney. The top non-commissioned officer in the entire United States Army. He wields or did wield a lot of power and influence. McKinney was the supreme enlisted leader of the Army. Or was he? In 1998, McKinney went to courts martial for multiple offense of sexual harrassment, lying during the investigation and subrogation of perjury. The Sergeant Major of the Army was convicted. In the U.S. Army, McKinney was suppose to exude leadership and I would imagine that the majority of the time he probably did. However, he became obsessed with his power of position and allowed his guttural desires for sex to overcome every other responsibility that he and his position required. Then, when caught, instead of stepping up and admitting his wrongful conduct, he lied and tried to get others to lie. What kind of message did McKinney send to tens of thousands of subordinates?

From the political set comes an example that is glaring in many ways. Al Lipscomb was a Dallas City Councilman. Lipscomb was a hell raiser, to say the least, and used his office as a pulpit to blast anyone that he perceived as anti-black, to attack the police with regularity, and to bolster his perceived position of leadership within the black community. Well, guess what? Al Lipscomb, the radicalized leader of the black community in Dallas and a growing following in other sections of the State, was really out for Al Lipscomb. He used his connections, his power, even his race, to feather his own bed. Al Lipscomb was arrested, tried and convicted on 96 counts involving the acceptance of bribes. What type of leader was he? What message to younger people or people who were interested in following him did Lipscomb send?

In Illinois, the Governor, George Ryan, the former Secretary of State of Illinois is being accused of involvement in a scheme of bribery that is ridiculous for its miniscule financial impact. So far, twelve officials of the Office of the Secretary of State have been indicted for accepting bribes from individuals who wanted to receive a commercial drivers license, to operate eighteen wheel truck tractor trailer rigs, but did not want to go through the legal processes to do so. Allegedly some of the bribe money paid found its way in to the election campaign coffers of the current Governor. What leadership!

The Attorney General of the United States, Janet Reno, has by all accounts of the many objective reports to date, used her position as the top law enforcement officer and prosecutor of this country to thwart the legal process of more than one political figure. The two most notorious are of course the President and Vice President of the United States. Now I am not going to re-live all of these scandals and shoddy conduct, but hundreds of Federal agents, career prosecutors of the Department of Justice, news media types, political figures and citizens at large cannot all be wrong in their judgements. The Attorney General has obstructed justice and utilized her position to provide "legalized" cover and semantic games to protect the two highest placed and criminally violative politicians in the land. What kind of leadership does she show? What will the future hold for those who thought they wanted to enter the DOJ and protect the country through the law? If we are a country of laws, which is open to serious debate, what has the Attorney General done to bolster that image?

When I was proudly, but naively, serving as a Deputy U.S. Marshal, I did not at first pay much attention to many things that went on around me, but through a persistence of conduct I began to open my glassy eyeballs and to take in what reality was all about. There was the supervisor in San Antonio, a married man, who had a pretty good looking girlfriend in El Paso who managed a Holiday Inn. Now the supervisor was one of those types we have all seen that had the swept back hair style and dressed pretty dapper. It was obvious that he featured himself as a lady's man. Well, whenever he got the "urge" he would use his position to usurp the known rotation schedules and would inject himself when it he wanted a government paid trip to frolic out west. It got to be a real sore point with personnel, but no one ever said anything, that I know of. What kind of leadership was that? Poor to be polite.

The last U.S. Marshal that I worked under was, without a doubt, the worst then, now, or even in the future. A man, no that is too good, a guy, who believed himself to be the savior of the profession. He went in for lots of "style", pomp and ceremony and expected everyone to fawn all over him. By the time he arrived on the scene I was the Deputy-In-Charge of the office in Del Rio. I had two other agents and we covered seven counties and three courts, along with a host of other duties. Went I was promoted to that position, the only other agent there was a retired Air Force NCO and much older than I. He did not cotton to my being placed in charge of the office. That presented difficulties and they only got worse when the second permanently assigned agent, another much older man, was transferred in. Well, regardless of the fact that I carried more than a third of the work load and did everything I could think of to operate fairly and to be supportive, it was not to be a close association. To make a long story short, I did not see it coming. Color me dumb, myopic, too trusting or whatever. At the close of one week San Antonio pulled the other two guys out for a "special assignment" and that would leave me to handle all the duties of the division, the next week, at least. Okay, but we had a ream of regulations on how we were to conduct those duties. One, that was to prove pivotal, was that we could not transport more than nine prisoners at a time in our vans, without a second agent. Friday afternoon I called and gave San Antonio a heads up on what I had layed on for the next week, particularly the numbers of prisoners to move, on that Monday, from Eagle Pass to Del Rio so that they could be picked up and moved by some-one else that same day and the next. I got no information. Then on the following Monday morning, before I set out for the day, I called again. This time I ask if they were sending me some assistance. I was told no. I reminded them about moving that many prisoners and the numbers for court. I was directed to do it anyway or incur the displeasure of the judges and the office in San Antonio. Well, needless to say, I did not see it com-ing. As it was to turn out, it did not make a difference what I did that day. I was in the proverbial spot and would have received a disciplinary action, no matter what. I just did not see it coming. So much for trust.

As it turns out, no matter what took place that day, I was a screwed goose and did not know it. I had to move thirteen. Guess what, between Eagle Pass and Del Rio, due to the weight, the van blew a tire. Now there I am, with thirteen in custody and four not shackled as we only had irons for nine, another part of the reason we were not to do what I was directed to do, and low and behold, everything went to the dogs, in a hurry. We did not have radios then and I had to unload to enable the changing of the tire. You guessed it, two of the four not in shackles took off through the tall and uncut for parts unknown. When I got to Del Rio I called and advised the Border Patrol and my office in San Antonio. San Antonio did not like the situation and immediately accused me of violating policy. No if's, buts, or maybe's, I was wrong. Okay, the stage was set. Within two weeks, and after burning a ton of personal hours on the investigation, and with some help from a couple of friends in other agencies, I got the two footloose and formerly free runners back. It made no difference. At the same time, I found out that my two personnel in the office had been filling the Marshal himself full of garbage about me. So my tenure became a target.

Now I have to admit that I did tweak the Marshal's beak pretty good on one occasion, but I honestly believe he ask for it. I had captured a young hispanic man with a small load of marijuana and put him in jail. The DEA and U.S. Attorney declined the case so I turned it over to the State. That was normal procedure. Only trouble was the young man was a nephew of a man who felt he was someone of importance. The uncle called the Marshal. The next thing I know the Marshal and his Chief Deputy, showed up unannounced in the office and wanted to talk, but not in the office. So we proceeded to the Marshal's motel room. That was a tip that something was up. Once inside, it became clear. I was to dismiss the case and I was not to make any further cases unless I obtained, in advance, the specific and personal permission of the Marshal himself. Now I am kind of hard headed at times and this was one of those times. I remember standing up and heading toward the door. The Marshal, a former shoe salesman and county employee, brusquely ask me if I understood his orders. I turned and stared him straight in the eye and told him "yes sir I do." Then I added, " if I see someone robbing the First National Bank I will go to a phone and call you and ask your permission to do something about it". Well, needless to say, that was not what he wanted to hear. Tough!!! What leadership. It wasn't too long after the prisoner deal, that I received a suspension. For years things had not been real good and I finally realized it. Then I was removed as the Deputy-in-Charge. This was all part of the Marshal's plan to get rid of those who he did not like and to replace them with his own followers. Leadership at its best!!

There are damn few that know this, but it bears revealing. That same Marshal came in to office shortly after some attempts on the life of an Assistant U.S. Attorney and threats surfaced against the life of U.S. District Judge John Wood. I served as the protective agent for both of those men. Well, the Marshal did not like the fact that so much of the budget was going to protect the judge and said so one day in a meeting with the judge. Judge Wood was a tough man and took no crud off anyone. He told the Marshal what he could do with the protection and so it was removed. Shortly after that, Judge Wood was assassinated. That act launched one of the largest and most protracted investigations up to that time. The FBI was in the lead, but many other agencies and officers were also involved. Every week there was a briefing held by the big wheels to review the case progress and to determine what to do next. It turns out that classifed information about the investigation was getting out on the street. Not good at all and was really making people mad. Then it was discovered who the leak was. The Marshal. To impress people with how much he knew, and thus to show off his power based on knowledge, he was running his mouth about the details of the investigation. There were those who wanted to indict him, but that was not seen as a good political move, so instead, they just cut him out of the loop. Another sterling example of his leadership and stupidity.

The dung heap was not smelling any more rosy and I decided that enough was enough. Besides, even though I had learned much and had experienced much, for which I was grateful, I knew that there had to be much more to the profession that I was not going to have access to and I wanted to continue to learn and grow. The future was not bright where I was, so I resigned and moved on. Only when I think about retirement, today, do I sometimes regret not having stayed in one place, because I could be retired. I can say, without a solitary doubt, that I learned some very important points about leadership. I learned more about what to do, and what not to do. The point being, you can even learn from the worst. For the remainder of the Marshals tenure and in to the next, the agency in the Western District had its problems. Why? Leadership, or rather the lack of positive leadership. Personnel will see what is going on and they pick up on it thinking if he can, I can.

In just a few weeks, I was back to work as an Agent with the State of Texas and the Texas Alcoholic Beverage Commission. At first I was stationed in

Dickinson and engaged in a wide variety of open and undercover work. It was new and exciting and my education continued. After a stint in Angleton, I was transferred, at my request to Mineral Wells. I was the only agent covering three counties. In meeting with the district supervisor I was told that there had not been any cases made in those three counties in a long time and that I was to go make them. Okay, I took the boss at his word. I met with the Chief of Police, the Sheriff, other officers, the DA and a host of others. I began my rounds and quickly learned that narcotics and violence in liquor establishments, bars and private clubs, was out of control. The Sheriff wanted action. In six months of long hours and hard work the list of investigations grew with rapidity. All the information went to Ft. Worth and there was not a single word of discontent coming back. The bar owners were getting the message. Shootings and stabbings in bars started to plummet. Narcotics violations were going elsewhere. The Sheriff and the DA were pleased as pigs in a new mud hole. Only trouble was, the owners of the bars were not pleased. Suddenly and with out warning, I was transferred to Amarillo. It seems the bar owners met with the agency director at a beer distributors meeting in San Antonio and complained mightily. I was out. The liquor industry ran the agency then and not the other way around. There were those officials who wrote letters and tried to stop this crass action, but to no avail. For me, well, it was a pain to say the least, but I knew I had done a good job and had nothing to be ashamed of. It was just another example of topsy turvy leadership.

In Amarillo, my reputation preceeded me. Not a bad one, just one of doing the job and not looking at who the offender was first. The District Supervisor there was an alcoholic to say the least. His main drinking buddy was the Sergeant. The Assistant District Supervisor was a nice, but fairly weak, individual who played the bureaucratic game everyday. Within six months of arriving I had been awarded a Meritorious Citation for the performance of duties above and beyond the call. I was proud of it, but had done what I believe anyone should have done. Then, the fecal matter hit the fan. The sergeant rode with me one night to see how I was working. Early in the morning he wanted to go to the office and we did. Now he coveted the Assistant District Supervisors position and with his relationship with the District Supervisor, everyone sort of wondered how long it would be before changes came. Well, this night, the sergeant went in the office and ask me to stand in the hall to watch the front door. The sergeant went to the locked door of the Assistant Supervisor and began to pick the lock. I was shocked to say the least and tried to figure out what the hell to do. I did not want to be a party to such a burglary and conduct unbecoming. I went in and sat at my desk in the squad room until he came out, and we left. That night I talked to my wife and tried to decide what the hell to do. Well, the arguments were short and there was only one action to take. The next morning I walked in and advised the Assistance District Supervisor as to what had transpired. Needless to say, he was ticked off. I left and went home as I was off duty.

Low and behold, shortly thereafter I was summoned to the District Supervisors office and given a letter of termination. The reason, I was a "disruptive influence".

Two days later the Assistant District Supervisor came to my home and gave me my final check and picked up some equipment. He told me how truly sorry he was, but he could not do anything about it. I learned later, that the District Supervisor was forced to retire and the Sergeant was transferred to the coast. After another screw up and he was busted in rank and on the next foul ball, they fired him. It hurt me financially and caused a great strain on my family, but I knew I had been right. It was sad beyond words that the local leadership and that in Austin, was so poor and even non-existent. Sure I could have kept my mouth shut, but then that would make me the punk of the Sergeant and no better than he was. That prospect did not intrigue me at all. His supervision and leadership were prompted by personal vindictiveness and the over riding desire to be promoted. He saw no wrong in his conduct to achieve his personal goals. Even the District Supervisor saw no wrong or chose to ignore it. There was another incident that drove home the mindset of this District

Supervisor. More than one agent had caught a particular package store selling booze after hours and to juveniles. In fact, there were a total of thirteen cases made, on the same place. Not a single one of those cases were ever sent to the DA's office. It turns out, the District Supervisor canned them all. Why? Oh, did I forget to mention that the store owner was responsible for paying for trips and other goodies for the District Supervisor? Illegal to say the least, but it was accepted as a way of doing business. Needless to say, that was not the only thing that I was privy to during my tenure with TABC, but somewhere you have to put things off, even though to the point and interesting, until another time. The foregoing is ample evidence of the corruption that consumed the agency, at least in those days.

Unfortunately, the few incidents revealed above are only the tip of the iceberg. There is not a day that goes by, that you can pick up a newspaper, or watch the television news or read a magazine that you will not learn of a new revelation about corruption and who is involved. The Justices of the Supreme Court of the State of New Hampshire are being investigated and possibly will be removed from office by the legislature. The highest judges, attorneys, in the State of New Hampshire caught up in an unexcusable scandal. Then you have the long running expose' concerning the rampant corruption of the Rampart Division of the Los Angeles Police Department. On top of that and on the opposite side of the country, there is the New York City Police Department. In between the two, there is Philadelphia, Chicago, Houston and others. With the exercise of just a little memory, we can quickly recall such debilitating conduct as that of U.S. Marine Corps Sergeant in Moscow, the CIA debacle involving the Ames', the Walker family of U.S. Navy fame, and a whole host of others. Having served as a Federal agent I know first hand many of the trust problems that other Federal agents speak of. Yet, the mindset of "we can't trust the locals" is not an honest position. Granted there is corruption all over the U.S. within local agencies, but there is not a Federal agency that I know of that has not had corruption themselves. That includes the FBI, the INS, the DEA, U.S.

Customs, the Border Patrol and others. Trust is something that you earn. It is not endowed just because of the source of the badge you wear or the position that one holds. Corruption erodes trust and re-building that trust is a long and difficult process. As for the often heard comment that you have to "play the game" and that it is a necessary evil of today's society, I can only reflect on what former President Andrew Jackson once uttered, "there are no necessary evils in government". History is replete with issues of ethical violations, criminality and a deficiency of integrity reaching into the most powerful hallways of America. Criminality is not limited to the homeless or the dope dealer or the 5th Ward in Houston. We have had such notables as John F. Kennedy, Edward Kennedy, Senator Packwood, Al Sharpton, and many of more recent vintage.

More recently Paul Begala, a former adviser to the President Clinton, made the statement that Clinton and the majority of his generation are the most self-centered and self-indulgent in history. Begala, while in the White House, was an unabashed defender of Clinton, and even now, still supports him for the most part. The commission of illegal and unethical acts, especially by those individuals who lead our nation are inexcusable, but when they are caught and continue to lie only worsens the original offense. In fact, sometimes, the actions to cover up misconduct is often more serious than the original misconduct. On March 29, 2000, during a news conference at the White House, President Clinton was answering a question unrelated to any one of his scandals, but in response to that question he stated "whatever the law is…we should obey it" and then stated "if somebody does something wrong, throw the book at them". Ludicrous comes to mind. Appalling would describe his audacity to believe that everyone in the country and acquired amnesia since his escapades and now he can speak those words with such sincerity. It just shows that people will say anything, at any given time, in order to advance their own agenda. The acceptance of responsibility for misconduct has become passe and like the French proverb says, "a fault denied is twice committed".

Leadership can be for good or for bad. The leader has to display ethical, moral, and consistent conduct. The leader has to be honest, not only with his subordinates, but with those they serve. That includes the public. Leaders who engage in misconduct and show that they cannot be trusted only serve to negatively influence those who work with or under them. At the same time, notable leaders adversely influence the public they serve. When misconduct goes unpunished or is extended over time, many will acquire the attitude that if he can do it and get away with it, then why shouldn't I do the same. It becomes infectious. As for the public, they have slowly, creepingly, been exposed to a continuous barrage of corruption on the part of officials and in so doing have just as slowly become used to that corruption. I do not consider this to be an over statement, but our society is awash with corruption. Corruption, in all of its hideous forms, on any level and in any profession is now viewed as business as usual. It now takes acts of corruption, which are more immense than those, which preceded, to even be reported, reviled or worried about.

Harry Truman, former President of the United States, was a politician, but he did make at least one statement that I can definitely agree with. Truman stated that "in periods where there is no leadership, society stands still". Leadership is a learned art form and when subordinates or citizens are provided with repetitious and negative leadership, they learn. What they learn, they pass on. Yet, as we will all see later in this book, even with the display of positive leadership, there are individuals who have become so accustomed to other manners of doing things that they resist the positive leadership in an attempt to continue their corrupt ways. Financially, there is no doubt, most of the time, that corruption pays better, but in the end it will cost a hell of a lot more than being honest.

FOR MANY PEOPLE, ETHICS IS SOMETHING YOU SELL.

The Author

CHAPTER FOUR

MIRRORS

Far too many officials, at all levels, believe, as does a great percentage of the general populace, that it is easier to climb a tree and tell a lie, than to stand on the ground and tell the truth. Sooner or later, the truth will come out and then the stories really get imaginative. Before it is over, the situation is far worse than it was in the beginning.

Fault? Where do we apply it? Who should shoulder the responsibility for corruption within the police profession? Do we tag only the officer that is caught?

Do we get the sergeant, the lieutenant, the Chief? Do we go after the mayor and city council? Do we blame "society" and attach all form of excuses and reasons why the poor flatfoot stepped over the line? Well, there is always enough "blame" to go around, but those most adept at escape and evasion are generally the ones that come out unscathed. However, there is one harbor of illegality, corruption, misconduct and unethical action that is rarely labeled as a participant in this sickening course of events. THE PUBLIC!

That is right. John Q Citizen, whether white, black, brown, yellow, red or polka dotted has to carry a chunk of the responsibility. Corruption is a process of gradual erosion. It is not an instantaneous or spontaneous event. In one city that I personally know, the police department or rather the so called Chief and Assistant Chief hand out Police Officer badges (reserves) and identification cards like they were tickets to a concert. All you have to be is black, influential or a hell raiser and you can have one. When you have it, like many have done in the past, you can flash it for free food, to get out of a traffic citation and a host of other little tidbits of favortism. In return you are to support the Mayor that is in office, for without him, the "kind officers" who gave you the badge will be gone, thus your "pass" will be taken up and revoked. Does the Mayor know this? Well, does a wild bear use the half moon facilities in the woods? It is a corrupt quid pro quo. The Mayor stays in office, thus the Chief stays in office, thus the Assistant Chief stays in office, thus the vote providers keep their influence and thus the Mayor stays in office. Around and around they go. One dirty hand washing the other.

After being forced out of the TABC I spent many hours second guessing myself and my actions. I finally beat myself up enough and realized that I had not done anything wrong. Yes, I was out of a job and that hurt, and I knew that the termination would not bode well for me in the near future, but I also knew that I would find another position. My father told me, on more than one occasion, that doing right was not always the easiest thing to do, but it was also the only thing to do. Brother was he right. Now you would think that such undesirable situations would be few and far between. If you do, then you would also be wrong. I too, at that point in time, believed the same way, but I was about to get round three.

After sending out a box full of resumes, I received an interview for the Chief of Police position with the City of Hico. A sleepy little town in east central Texas. With a population of just under two thousand it should have been fairly easy and with little if any problems. Guess again. I was appointed Chief and for the first two months I lived in a motel. Granted the pay was lower than a snake's belly in a wagon rut, but I was working in my chosen profession. The department had two officers, three old patrol units, and a hole in the wall office. The nearest jail belonged to the county, twenty miles away. The city was made up primarily of senior citizens, but there was a young and rather unruly set that controlled the city after dark. In fact they would block off the downtown streets and drink, shot out the lights, break windows and engage in various acts of carnal knowledge. This was a tough crowd, belonging to the rancher set mostly, and not in the mood for caring a twit about anyone else. Granted, there was almost nothing for them to do and that made things difficult, but that became an excuse and not a valid reason. The two officers were basically lazy, poorly trained, total non-motivated and disrespectful of the very law they represented. The one I referred to as Howdy Doody, from the early television days, was the worst. He fancied himself as an expert on everything. When I went home to bring my wife and children down the mice began to play. When I got back I learned that these two paragons of policing had been drinking beer on duty and in uniform and in the patrol unit, downtown with the tough guys. Now that won't do, but even worse was the fact that their beer drinking buddies had pulled them out of the patrol unit, through the windows, took their sidearms away from them, and sent them home on foot. I was not a happy camper to say the least. I doesn't take a genius to figure out what I did in response. They were terminated, but that wasn't the end of it. That very night the tough guys and girls decided to take over. About 8:00 PM I contacted the Sheriff's Office and the Highway Patrol and got them to come up for a night exercise in crowd control. The message to the jerks was clear the street or go to jail. I even went to the mayor's house and got him to come see how these "misunderstood" darlings were acting. They were mad that their drinking buddies were fired and wanted them back. Did they want them back because I was wrong? No. they wanted them back because they knew they could do whatever they wanted and these two idiots would not stop them.

The senior citizens liked the peace and quiet that followed, but there were regular encounters along the way. Yet, that is only the most immediately noticeable problem confronting this city. When you drive in to the city, to this day, or at least the last time I was there a couple years ago, you approach a Y in the highway. On the left side of the Y was a small café named the Koffee Kup Kafe. Quaint? Family run and the food was not all that bad. However, not everything is as it may appear. The café was actually a KKK setting? In fact, Hico was the seat of long standing center for right wing white supremacist. Every year, the KKK from all over the U.S. gather in the City Park for speeches and then they burn a cross and have more speeches on private land just south of town. For almost ten years I had been collecting information about terrorism and white supremacy and broadening my expertise in that field and low and behold I was sitting right slap dab in the middle of a nest of pointy hat guys. Now all of this was bad enough, especially for a guy who was in his first position as Chief and wishing he could find a place of peace and quiet to work in, but as I have learned, every city has its "touchables", or so they think.

On Halloween, kids will be kids, but these not so young kids were really pressing the envelope. By now I had been able to employ a couple of better personnel and was sitting at home. Unfortunately, things were not to remain even half quiet. It seems that a councilman's 16 year old daughter and some others got together for the forceful exchange of frozen water balloons. That went on until the new wore off and they looked for another target. They selected an eighteen wheel truck tractor trailer that was passing through the city and threw two of these frozen greetings through the drivers window. The lady operating the rig was a damn good drivers and was able to get the rig stopped just a few feet from running over the two gas pumps at the closed gas station. I hate to think of what would have happened had she not been able to control that monster of a vehicle. Most of the kids got caught before I got there, and the case was handled like any other. The flak that it generated was yet to come. To make a long story short, the councilman, who was also the police commissioner for the city, raised a ruckus and that led to a special meeting of the council. At that meeting I was ordered to destroy the case file and all the statements and other documents. That was illegal. I told the mayor I could not destroy it so I was ordered to provide the file to him. That I did, then it disappeared. Now I was not surprised. However, the county District Attorney and the Grand Jury got wind of the dealings and the investigation was on. There was seven very upset souls when they got subpoenaed to the grand jury to explain what, why, and when. Of course, no one got indicted, but the handwriting was on the wall for me. Luckily I found a DA that was looking for someone of integrity to be his investigator and we hit it off. I resigned and my family and I got the heck out of that burg. I have heard much about it in the following years, and most of it was not good. I periodically went back to the KKK meetings and collected more and more information. Two mayors later, I was ask to come back and respectfully declined.

During that almost two years I was regularly challenged physically, my home was the object of attack, and my car was vandalized. While the senior citizens, of whom there were many, sent me notes and cards of thanks and publicly berated the council for my leaving, the rest were glad to see me go. They obviously wanted things to be the way they used to be, wide open. For the next several years, they got exactly that. This is a classic example of how a sect of society comes to believe that they are immune to the rigors of the law that they want everyone else to be subject to. Before, some during, and after my tenure, they got exactly what they wanted and paid for. Of course, being a site of homage for the Klan and the many offshoot organizations did not exactly help their reputation, but then the local affiliation was much stronger than they wanted anyone from the outside to know. Today, as I understand, the police force is much more professional and used the foundation I laid to build a department which is greatly more respected.

There is no denying that I am a candid spoken individual. Some would be less gracious and say that I am just plumb blunt. That may be, but one

thing is for sure, if you don't want to know the straight answer to something, don't ask me the question. When I get up in the morning I have a
ritual like everyone else for preparing for the days events. One of the first
tasks is to scrape off the growth of beard to try and make myself more
handsome. I know, it is a lost cause, but then it doesn't hurt to try. For all
the trials and tribulations that I have been through in my career, and for
all the upheavals based on my standing up for what I believed in, I can
honestly state that I was never ashamed of what I saw in the mirror, so I
did not have to worry about cutting my own throat.

Hico was an education of another kind and could be a poster board for
what ails this nation. Those who were in control thought they were the
only ones who knew what as right, not only for themselves, but for everyone else as well. They used their elected positions to garner power and
then to exercise that power over others. By ignoring what was right and
needed, by causing officers to do things that were not within the bounds
of ethical conduct and by causing officers to suffer humiliation and coer-
cion, the leadership delivered the unmistakable message that misconduct
was acceptable. Over time, the repetition of that message was absorbed
by the officers and the self-indulgence of the city fathers engrained their
conduct and the subsequent conduct of the police. When the officers
openly engaged in unbecoming conduct, no one took any action to end
such conduct and to rectify a deteriorating situation. Those in the city
who saw the problems, were not in positions to cause any change and
even they, over time, came to accept the state of affairs. Thus for many
years the city and its controlling majority got exactly what they wanted
and what they paid for.

There are basically two types of city governments in Texas, and most
other states as well. One is the Mayor and Council form of government
and the other is the Manager and Council form. Now, some will argue that
the Mayor and council form is more responsive and responsible, while others would state that the Manager and council form places an individual of
non-political ties in the middle to impart impartial administration for all

the citizens. With a Mayor and council form of government the Mayor was the key figure and through appointments, finances and other means, wielded a lot of power. For a Chief of Police who could not or would not keep the Mayor happy, longevity was not extensive. Then, of course, the Manager was seen as a professional administrator and such conduct as experienced under a Mayor would not take place under the Manager. I remember attending a seminar in Dallas some years back where the major topic was employment of personnel, public administrative procedures and similar management topics. There were several city managers in attendance and serving on the panels. During one session the question was raised about city managers, Chiefs of Police, what managers looked for and what managers wanted. Now that is a bunch to talk about in a short period, but it was also a point of great interest. To a man, the city managers discussed how they sought men or women of integrity, of high ethical values, of principled leadership, of not wanting yes men, of wanting a person of skill and capability to relieve the city manager of having to deal with the day to day issues of the police department. They all wanted a good administrator. Now those few at this seminar may have been very serious in their beliefs and statements, but such a position, by most managers is about as foreign to their city as no strings attached Federal money.

In the last couple of years I have applied with somewhere between fifty and one hundred cities for the position of Chief of Police. My background is definitely not shabby and my successes have been many, yet whether the hiring official was a Mayor or a City Manager, the primary results were always the same. I can sum it up in the words of the former city manager for a city south of San Antonio. He was a retired Army Colonel from up north. Based on our conversations he and I saw things pretty much alike and would have made a good working team. I was his number one selectee for the position. However, the council and mayor were to make the final choice, and it turned out to be a man with no prior full time paid experience. When the city manager called me with the results, I ask him want had I done to cause me to lose the position. I was informed that it was not my fault. The manager stated that the council hired the other individual because they were afraid of me and that I would know more than they did. Now I had been told a lot of reasons why I did not get various jobs, but this was a new one and hard to swallow.

Yet, upon reflection, I realized that professional jealousy and fear of being revealed for someone of less than competent ability, could be their own logical reasoning for not wanting a trained and experience professional in the mix. It is still stupid, and I do not agree with such a notion, but I do understand it. The city manager lastly advised me, what was to be an even bigger shock, and that was that I should "dumb down" my resume.

For almost thirty years I have followed the advice of many in academia and law enforcement administration. That was to learn all you can, get your education and degrees, and to obtain all the training possible, so that you can achieve the highest level of competence and ability. Now, those goals have been achieved to a degree not possessed by the majority of my peers, and what has been the result. There are no doubts that some Mayors and City Managers seek to appoint and employ the best personnel they can attract, however, the majority within my experience and knowledge do not. In fact, while they espouse those goals in public and write their vacancy announcements to include those virtues, they do not practice them in the ultimate selection process. The words are part of the game. The overall game is control. To appoint and employ a Chief of Police with those attributes entails hiring a man or woman who is independent of mind, but not necessarily of team oriented management. To employ an individual of principle and ethics invites non-conformance with what they believe to be the best, even if not legal or ethical, course of action. The powers that be want someone whom they can control and manipulate. They want someone who knows the profession, but is possessed of a weaker will and will submit to the pressures of the politicians. My profession has seen many strong men and women, who did not adhere to such a whimsical standard and unfortunately they did not last long.

That is why the national average for tenure of a Chief of Police hovers around only twenty months.

Of course, the turnover in the top spot of an agency is not limited to just those Chiefs of substance. Over and over again, cities are required to seek a new Chief because the one they previously hired was not up to the task. Not just in playing the local games, but in administering an agency and abiding by the law and rectifying problems. So the less qualified get the job over the more qualified, but the less qualified inevitably causes the government entity more problems than they can control. So he is out and the search starts anew, but do most of the cities learn from their errors? No. They turn around and do the same thing all over again. And so it goes. In one eighteen month period, a city to which I had applied and lost out, hired and fired three Chiefs. The one who got the position when I applied was a patrol officer with no prior management experience and only four years total police experience. The next one was a sergeant within the same department who was related to a member of the council. The last one was a former Captain of reserves for the department down the highway, a city of far fewer citizens and problems. He too was never a full time officer and lacked any formal training necessary to be successful, but he was of the right race. Failure followed failure.

While serving the City of Hico I continued to look for a better opportunity and got the chance to compete for the same position with an upscale city north of Ft. Worth. This is one experience that is most indicative of what I have been discussing here. The city manager was in his sixties if he was a day. He wanted to meet my wife also, so on the appointed day we drove up and got to his office about fifteen minutes early. For the next forty-five minutes we sat and waited. The manager was late for the appointment and that was not a good sign. Upon being invited in to his office by the secretary, we walked to his desk and he did not look up, nor did he stand up to shake my hand or to be courteous to my wife. That was two more less than encouraging indicators. So far he was not impressing me at all, but I decided to see where this would all lead. Without any pleasantries or introductions he began to tell me about how long he had been in city government and what he felt a police department should do and be. I was given a long tirade about his personal expertise and knowledge in managing and knowing what a department should and should not do. There was no questions, just stiff pronouncements. He was going to dictate how many citations were written, who would be arrested, days off for personnel, the budget, training and on and on. I finally got a word in edge wise and ask him, if the Chief of Police was going to be in charge of the department or was he. I knew it was not a question to ask that would engender his approval, but I had sat through enough. His reply was, "I am going to have a great say in what is done". I stood, followed by my wife, and told him that he did not need me and we walked out. So much for that job. Shortly thereafter, he hired a female officer as Chief from within the department. In less than a year the department was embroiled in a controversy surrounding favortism and sexual misconduct within the agency. Not to mention the lack of ability for investigating a high profile homicide. So she was out. The city manager was soon given the gate and the city was back to square one. All because one man felt he was so damn smart and possessed unchallenged power. This is another example of how control is a primary concern of those in power. If they lose control, or so they perceive, they lose that power. I would not have lasted a week with a person of his nature. Overall, the agency suffered very badly. The city took a pounding in the media. The citizens really lost respect and confidence in the police. Yet, unless everyone was deaf, dumb, blind and stupid, someone knew what was going on, but chose not to intervene. So it can be argued that the citizens, once again, got what they deserved and or wanted.

Then there was Red Oak. A small but growing community north of the metroplex, that had a lot of potential. Once again, my background elevated me to a slot among those finalist to be interviewed. I have always tried to get to the potential new city early enough to look around and to try and find out as much as the city and the department as I could before going in to an interview. I looked on such an effort as trying to gain an edge in the information area. On this occasion I stopped at the local Dairy Queen and wound up meeting a Deputy Sheriff. In the converation I was told how tightly the Mayor liked to control things and that while the department was small, it had huge problems. He would give not real specifics, but the tone of the situation was unmistakable. So it was no surprise when I entered the room of the interview and felt the tensions between the mayor and his clique and the opposing force of two councilmen. You could cut it with a knife.

The interview went along without a hitch until the inevitable question arose. The mayor inquired if I agreed that it would be in the city interest to not take all driving while intoxicated offenders to jail, but rather, for the officers to take them home. Now this is a question that is loaded with ambiquity and really cannot be answered honestly, if you intend to fill the position. In fact, it is a flat out trap.

Well, having had that question poised before, I knew my answer, but I also knew that the position just went south. I advised the mayor that such a practice would be detrimental. I inquired as to who was going to establish the list of names of individuals who would be "taken home"? Who would be the individual to be called at 2:00 A.M. by the officer, to ascertain if an individual, not on the list, should be on the list? Did the city insurance cover an officer who relied on such a list and then was sued for discriminatory conduct for complying with the list? Did the city insurance cover all cost of medical care and even lose of life should an accident take place while the "listed individual" was being transported home in a city patrol unit? Needless to say, the answers, or rather the lack of answers were there own answers.

I knew the results to come and was resigned to having wasted my time and money in pursuit of this position. Upon being politely thanked for my attendance, I started to exit the room and was stopped by the only black city councilman, and obvious opponent of the mayor. He extended his hand and shook mine, saying, I want to thank you for being so honest. It was refreshing. Granted, that would be little consolation, but then again, he did not have to take the initiative. So, my list of experiences grew and I tried to decide if I had been wrong in vocalizing such a position. In the end, my answer was no. I could not remember who said it, but someone back in time the words had been uttered, which remained just as true now as they had been when first spoken. If you don't stand for something, you will fall for anything. That may not be completely accurate, but it is close enough to impart the meaning and it is damn sure true.

It is sort of humorous, in a sad way, but as the years roll by, the public and far too many public servants, never seem to catch on. I would be willing to bet that I have heard John, or Jane, Doe citizens complain hundreds, if not thousands, of times that they can no longer trust the police, or the police or corrupt, or the police don't know what they are doing, or that politicians are only out for themselves, and on and on. Even, in the immediate past months of this writing, the news media types have interviewed citizens about the Presidential Election and repeatedly citizens have stated that they do not believe that politicians can be trusted. Well, just who is abdicating their responsibilities? Is the police officer who is involved in corruption? Absolutely! Is the politician? You bet! Are the whining, crying, moaning and groaning citizens? Without a doubt! For in the final analysis, the citizens are in control, even if they don't remember what their Civics teacher taught them. In point of fact, the ultimate responsibility for what happens in our society belongs to those who live in our society—the citizens. I remember an example that is dead on point. The District Attorney of the 35th Judicial District was making final arguments to a jury of twelve men and women in a major felony case. As he began to close off his remarks, he paused, placed his hands on the rail separating him from the jury box, looked up and down the two rows of jurors, and then made a statement that has stuck with me, and hopefully others that heard it, for all the ensuing years. The District Attorney stated, "We have all heard individuals complain about the criminal justice system. Everyday, people make the comment, 'they don't do anything to anyone down at the courthouse'. Well, today, you are the they. You must decide". It was a crushing and true argument and its effect was undeniable. In those few well chosen words, one man, who believed in the sanctity of the system and the integral nature of the citizens role in that system, hit the nail squarely on the head.

Every morning when I get up, to go to work or to look for work, I have to face myself in the mirror. For all the trials and tribulations, for all the mistakes I have made, for all the anguish I have put my family through due to my choice of occupations, and for all the troubles that have accompanied my decisions, I am not ashamed of what I see in that mirror. Nor am I ashamed of the reflections generated by the mirrors of my mind and the memories of thirty years behind the badge. Sure, on some occasions, I would have, in retrospect, done a few things differently, but when it came down to doing the right thing or the wrong thing, the outcome would have been the same. Cities, Counties, States, organizations, agencies and other entities, all too often, are only mirrors, which reflect the attitudes, sentiments and wants of the public. So if you don't like the image you see, get a new mirror or clean the one you have.

Political egoism has ruined many good law enforcement agencies
and individuals.

Author

Chapter Five

Contentment

I had achieved one dream of being a Federal agent, but it was not as lofty as I had envisioned it would be. I had worked undercover in the State and against the Louis Beams of this land, and that was good. I had served as a Chief of Police, which was another dream, and it definitely was not all it was cracked up to be. One goal I sought was to become one of the best investigators in the business and the opportunity for that achievement was yet to come. In January of 1985 I met and talked with the District Attorney of the 35th Judicial District, the Honorable Steve

Ellis, of Brownwood, Texas. Here was a tall and bright individual with a winning personality. Ellis was looking to employ an investigator in his office. It was to my great fortune that I was selected. So I bid Hico farewell and moved my family to the center of Texas. It was to be a period of accomplishment, of some anguish, and of more contentment that previously experienced as a law enforcement professional.

My knowledge base would grow by leaps and bounds. I developed expertise in more than one area, not possessed by many. My success in investigations became somewhat expected and my reputation also grew.

In the ten years to follow I can honestly say that I really made a difference. A good difference. Yet, the ugly side followed also. Well, that is not exactly true. It did not follow me, as I was not leading the uglies, and it did not precede me in anticipation of my arrival. I slowly began to realize that the uglies existed everywhere. Even though I continued to hold to that somewhat naïve attitude that police and public servants were suppose to be honest and could be trusted. From the beginning I was determined to present the best image, the best qualities and the best work, and to get along with everyone. I was the new kid, so to speak, on the block and wanted to step slowly, but firmly, and earn the respect of those I would be working with and for. Now, a District Attorney Investigator has statewide authority and can have a tremendous impact on the criminal cases, as well as victims, attorneys, agencies and other officers. In many jurisdictions the DA Investigator works all types of cases from complaint to trial, while in other jurisdictions, they do mostly follow up work after another agency has completed the investigation. I was fortunate to work for an office that wanted the whole enchilada. From soup to nuts and everything in between. That was what I was hoping for and right down my alley. Heaven was definitely smiling on me and utopia had been found. Well, almost.

I set about meeting all the local officials or being introduced to them by the DA at various functions. Yet, there were two that would never be very warm and would ultimately, be a royal pain.

There are two aspects of life and the law enforcement profession that I was about to begin a long introduction to. Those are control and professional jealousy. Now you may think that control would be a pertinent topic, but what in blazes does professional jealousy have to do with anything. Well, welcome to the real world and read on.

Within a week of arriving in Brownwood the Sheriff of Brown County called the office and wanted to know if I was available to be shown around the county and to go to lunch. Obviously, this was a sojourn that was expected and should go a long way to establishing that good working relationship that I desired and that would be beneficial to everyone. You bet'cha. Sheriff Bill showed up at the appointed hour and we were off. We drove south out of town and in a meandering route, ultimately traversing some back country roads and trails, the whole time the Sheriff was talking non-stop. Mostly, he was "acting" like a tour guide, but it soon became apparent that this was not a tour and a professionally friendly gesture to the new man in town. The truth came out, ever so subtly, when the Sheriff made the comment that he was the top law enforcement officer in the County and that things worked better when any work anyone was doing went through him. I thought to myself, really. What about the Chief of Police and the Brownwood PD, the DPS, and all the others, do they go through you. Yet, not wanting to immediately upset his apple cart, I just listened. We did not get back to town until almost five that afternoon, and I was worn out, especially my ears. The upshot of this venture into interpersonal communications was this, the Sheriff was trying to covertly tell me that my existence and future would be much better if everything I was to do as the DA Investigator was cleared through the Sheriff in advance. I honestly believe that the Sheriff featured himself as the top dog in the county and gave little consideration to the position of the District Attorney. One would immediately wonder what was going on and what was the Sheriff involved in that he worried about someone else undertaking an action that might threaten him and or his position. Was he accepting bribes, involved in narcotics, covering for illegal conduct, or what? I did not bust his bubble, but the die had been cast and could only forebode bad times to come.

The other less than sterling figure to become involved in this messy mix was the slow footed and dim witted future Chief of Police. Now the Chief in Brownwood is elected, thus it is a popularity contest. I first met Joe when I taught a seminar at Tarleton State University on Terrorism, while I was the Chief in Hico. He slept most of the time. With an intellect as dull as a rock, his only chance to rise up in the ranks was by playing the local games. It sure was not based on brillance, innovation, effectiveness or leadership. Don was the present Chief and not a bad guy. He had problems within the department and outside, but was not really hard to get along with. Don was no fan of the Sheriff and I could understand why. Here is where we can explore the first of the two realities, control.

As previously mentioned, the Sheriff wanted to control it all. The why would become evident as time went on.

The case work was steady, mostly low grade, but punctuated with high profile investigations. It could take several volumes to discuss the myriad of cases that I was involved in, but we will limit the exploration to those that generated the most attention and the most problems. These will focus on a major gambling operation, widespread narcotics, the KKK and associates, Capital Murders (that is plural) and bank robbery.

In this day and time gambling is as common among our citizenry as bad breathe, baldness and disrespect. Everyone thinks that they can hit it big. Lots of money for little or no work. This is the mentality that keeps the casinos in Las Vegas and Atlantic City thriving. Joining this search for wealth has been a flood of casinos opened on Indian Reservations. Even the Kickapoo's have gotten into the act with a hole in the wall operation located out in the sticks of Maverick County. For the big boys in Las Vegas and Atlantic City, they have made billions and will make billions more. For the native Americans they want to make millions and millions. For those who go to "play", they too want to make millions, but it rarely works that way. All across America and in most foreign nations there are those enterprising souls who want to make millions, but do not want to expend or can't afford to expend the millions to do it within the legally established framework. These gamblers run what is known in the parlance as "books" or "numbers". They are illegal, but many of them are raking in millions illegally. Just as the Mafia, they have it down to a science.

Well, Brownwood had its own gambling sect. The book was owned and operated by Bobby. Bobby booked bets from just about anyone on sports games, primarily basketball and football. I got wind of the operation from a disgruntled player and former friend of Bobby. It took a few months of work, and I won't go in to the details as it would take much too long, but we finally collected enough information and probable cause to obtain numerous search warrants. Now, we knew from the investigation that there would be some police individuals involved, so we had to be particularly careful about releasing information. On the appointed day that we intended to bring the case down, we had obtained six search warrants for six separate locations. It would be tricky, but if we handled it right, all would go well. The DA, his assistant Fred Franklin, and I sat down and drew up a list of those officers we could depend on. We put one of them in charge of each search warrant. The Chief and Sheriff were called and given a general run down, but no names were mentioned. We ask for all the personnel they could provide. A briefing was held with all participating officers in attendance. A couple tried to use the pay telephone to make calls just prior to our leaving, but somehow or other, is was out of order.

All the warrants were executed simultaneously and brother did the roaches head for cover. At the same time, the media spotlight was glaring and when the names involved were learned by the citizens, the phones started ringing. The confidential source had overseen a major business in Brownwood and was in dire financial straits, not to mention other serious troubles. This individual had laid out the entire floor plan of the operation and provided details of telephone conversations and transactions which were invaluable.

The amount of evidence seized was tremendous, but the items that would ultimately lead to the treasure trove and convictions were a group of little spiral bound books. I had called in two friends from the IRS office in Abilene early on and they were present on the raids. For the next few weeks we spent thousands of hours going through these books. In just over two years, the book making operation had over ten million dollars go through it. Bobby, a former upstanding coach type in the area, was making a bunch of money. Needless to say, he had no Federal gambling tax stamp and had not declared any of his "gains" on his income tax. Most of the names in the books were coded, but with relentless analysis and hundreds of other documents we figured them all out. Then came the subpoenas to appear before the Grand Jury. Doctors, Attorneys, Teachers, businessmen, Dentist, a Judge, and the list goes on. They were not happy campers to have their names associated with this organized criminal activity and to be facing criminal charges. The Sheriff, well he was upset to say the least. Other officers were upset. Not at the ones caught or the fact that such a major illegal operation was being conducted. They were upset at me. Before it was all over, several participants decided that it would be in their best interest to cooperate. The book was busted up, monies seized, equipment and records seized, and convictions had. It was a damn good piece of law enforcement work, but the general feeling was not congratulatory. Those involved, of position or not, had been caught in corruption, including a number who felt they were above the law. The DA and his Assistant had steered the operation and deserve a lot of the credit for cleaning the situation up. They also stood behind me. As for IRS, well a pig in a new mud hole could not have been more pleased. Yet, I had to suffer the slings and arrows from fellow officers in the area, but I chalked it up to the source.

I was learning how to conduct the most major of investigations and I worked at it relentlessly. My skills were growing and it was becoming obvious to many through the results acquired. Yeah, that sounds egotistical, but the truth is the truth. The court reporter for the 35th District Court remarked one afternoon that he would hate to have me on his trail. Such words did not go to my head, but were gratifying.

Now it was obvious that I was not ever going to be the most favorite police officer in Brown County, because of my work and refusal to "play the game", but it was also becoming obvious that more and more were beginning to realize that a new brand of law enforcement was in town and knew what to do. For the Chief in the adjoining city of Early, Chuck we will call him, I was not a man to be cooperated with or associated with.

Chuck was short, fat, and stupid, but liked to try and convince everyone that he knew it all. After a few less than courteous comments by him, the relationship was forever ruined, but then what little control he had was easily skirted. That brings up the next debacle by the locals.

On going to my bank one day, which was located in Early, I spoke to a couple of the ladies there who I considered friends and during that conversation one of them mentioned a hole in the bottom of the front window. I looked at it and became very curious. It was a bullet hole, located just a couple inches above the floor and the bullet had entered from the outside. They did not know where the expended round was. It could have come from any number of weapons and shooters for any number of reasons, but there was something that nagged at me about it. Nothing happened for several weeks. Then, on my way in to the office early one morning, I drove by the Early Bank and there was a crowd of police and others gather around. I went back and found out that the bank had been robbed during the night. That someone had knocked a hole in the front door glass just above the frame, a few inches above the ground, and had placed what was suppose to be a remotely controlled explosive device, contained in a brown paper bag, inside the door, on the floor. An Early PD officer found the situation. The requested funds were removed from the vault and given to the officer, as the accompanying note demanded. The officer said that a voice on top of the building told him to throw the money up on the roof and to leave.

Chief Chuck did not want me to dismantle the alleged explosive device, even though he knew I was a bomb technician. In fact, he said no police trusted me. More of his moronic ramblings. Chief Don and I went in. I had called the FBI office in Abilene and learned that Mike Morris, with whom I had worked many cases, was on his way. This whole thing stunk to high heaven. The explosive device was a hoax.

When the FBI arrived, we commenced the investigation and within two hours Mike and I both agreed the story of the police officer just would not work. There were no marks on the outside of the building where someone got up and down from the roof. The roof was not disturbed. The considerable sum of money and the brown paper bag were gone. It was time to tear the story apart. The target was the Early PD officer. That did not make Chief Chuck, the Sheriff and some others happy. Within a short amount of time, the officer was telling more stories than Carter's had pills. Bits and pieces of incriminating information came out and there was no doubt that the police officer had committed the act. The patrol unit was searched, the tire tool used to break the window seized and glass fragments recovered. On a hunch, we took the robbery demand note to the Early City Hall. There was only one copying machine which was used by all the employees, including the Police Department. We obtained numerous copied pieces of paper from the machine, without duplicating any document. A cursory examination showed the same "trash" marks on the copies we made that were on the piece of paper containing the robbery demand note. These went to the lab in D.C. and came back a perfect match.

I remembered the bullet hole in the window and now we knew what it was about. It was a test to see if the windows were wired to the alarm. The Officer had been carefully planning this action, but not carefully enough. For all the heat and accusations sent in my direction, the Officer went to Federal court in San Angelo and received a three year prison sentence. Another officer had stepped way over the mark, for personal gain, and then went to extraordinary lengths to try and divert the attention of all on the ones that had caught him. Chief Chuck, well, he looked bad, but turned his vindictiveness on me. The Sheriff, well, it just added to his dislike and that situation would not get better.

By this time, there were those wearing badges that felt that I was some kind of little tin god trying to save the world. That was an undeserved claim and I have to admit it cut down on my inter-actions and it did wear on me personally, but I knew that right was right. There were many citizens and officials that stated their appreciation in private, but would not go public.

Now, Brownwood and Brown County were not unlike nearly every other city and county in the United States. Drugs, illicit narcotics, were there and the business was pretty good. The number of dealers would have filled a small telephone book. On behalf of the DA, and in opposition to the Sheriff, I testified at a meeting of the area council of governments in favor of creating a regional narcotics task force. The Sheriff opposed the idea. The Task Force was created and I served on the Board of Directors. At the same time, I got the DA to agree to form a three man team to work narcotics within the two counties of the Judicial District. I got one detective from the PD and, reluctantly, one Deputy from the Sheriff's Office. We spent hundreds of thousands of hours, collecting intelligence, interviewing arrestees, developing informants, identifying dealers and conducting investigations. It was not to go for naught. Five methamphetamine labs were busted. Dozens of dealers were caught in undercover buy operations and even a favorite watering hole in one section of the city was ultimately bulldozed as a nuisance. Caught up in these far ranging dragnets were a bunch of dope dealers and users. A few traffickers running the junk in to town and to surrounding areas were taken down. There was a couple of attorneys, a raft of high school students, and a jail full of scum bags whose only source of income came from dope. This effort went on for about two years, until the Sheriff wanted his man back and other demands of manpower brought out efforts to a slow pace. Oh, did I mention that the daughter and son-in-law of the Sheriff were popped? More than once? They were and there was no cover from certain areas for them to hide under. The Sheriff made calls to the DA. The Sheriff was catching hell from his wife. Deputies were afraid to say anything or even to be seen near me. Had the girl been caught once, well no one would have said a thing, if she had gotten a slap on the wrist, but after the first one, came another, and another. She was a slow learner. The Sheriff just refused to accept the obvious, but couldn't find a way to stop it, either her or the DA office. Needless to say, that ripped it. Sheriff Bill and his supporters grew to hate the DA and myself and we would never exchange even the remotest of casual comments in the future. I honestly felt for the guy. He was in one damn tough position, but his wife and his daughter and others should have known better. He sure should have. Yet, he forfeited his trust and respect within the law enforcement profession for expedience and family. The other way would have been very hard, but then doing right often is hard. Overall, the dope business in Brownwood went down like a rock and with the clean up of areas of the city many citizens were pleased as peaches. We had done a good job.

During the ten years I worked as an investigator for more than one District Attorney, there were a number of real big cases. Some of them generated difficulties as we have seen, but difficulties also arose from the unlikely little cases. I spoke to the State Crimestoppers Association in Garland not to long ago and ask how many people would pay any attention to a little old lady of obvious demented capacity when she wanted to make a complaint. Surprisingly, most said they would not and yet, it was not surprising. I learned early on that many law enforcement personnel fail to listen to people and offhandedly refuse to believe citizens when it sounds too far fetched. From personal experience, I have found that you should never blow someone off just because it seems to be implausible.

This next case is a prime example. An elderly man and woman called the DA office and wanted someone to help them get their savings back. They had given about seven thousand dollars to a man to invest. Needless to say, the man and their money went south. I went out to Bangs, Texas to interview them and see what could be done. Within minutes of them initiating what would be a long and rambling story, I realized that a scam artist alleging to be an investor was on the loose in the area. Backtracking and sharing information with other agencies, talking to a friend at the SEC and working with an investigator for the State Board of Securities, we got an identification on the scam and the con man running it. It took a few months to nail it all down, but success did come. The Sheriff's office had blown the elderly couple off and would not help them. In Oklahoma City, the court convicted the crew of scam artists and put them in prison.

The defense attorney, attempting to buy mercy for the culprits sent the DA office a certified check for $7000. The smile and hug that I got when I returned their money will never be forgotten by me. The mutterings and dislike emanating from the Sheriff were hurtful and mis-directed, but were far outweighed by the appreciation shown by the elderly citizens that we had helped.

For seven good years I worked in the office of the District Attorney in Brownwood, Texas. The first DA was Steve Ellis and when Steve went back to private practice, he was followed by his assistant Fred Franklin. Both of these men were top drawer and we remain friends to this day. Unfortunately, all good things come to an end and Fred lost the next election to the former County Judge. It did not take long for the word to get back to me. The Sheriff, who could not force his influence on Steve and Fred, did get to Lee. The Sheriff agreed to throw his political influence to the challenger for the DA office, if when elected, the new DA would eliminate the position of investigator within the office of the DA. Lee needed all the help he could get, and they struck a bargain. So, I looked around and found a DA in the Panhandle who wanted an investigator and went to work for him. After the Sheriff in Brown County had to step down, the newest DA re-instituted the investigator position. Politics does make for strange bedfellows. Oh, I wonder what influence the unsavory activities of the new DA and his wife might have had on their relationship with the Sheriff and the agreement? Before leaving this part of the history, I want to state that there was a number of police officers and other officials who were bent clean out of shape. Their corrupt conduct was inexcusable. However, there were also a larger number of individuals within the city and county who were straight as a string, but were afraid of saying or doing anything out of fear of losing their jobs. There were a few others that skated on the edge and while they did not engage in illegal activities, they did participate in conduct that was at the very least, unethical.

When I attended the first class of the Law Enforcement Management Institute of Texas (LEMIT), beginning in 1989, the focus of this Texas equivalent to the FBI National Academy and similar institutions, was to be on the knowledge and skills that managers and administrators would need to provide positive direction to any type of law enforcement agency. For ten months, we received very high quality instruction from professors and practitioners from Texas A&M University, Texas Woman's University and Sam Houston State University. This was graduate level work and well worth the effort. One of the professors that worked with us was Sam Souryel, a former Egyptian military officer and police officer. His specialty was Police Ethics. It has been, was then and continues to be a very hot and timely topic.

We have all heard the jokes about police officers and doughnuts and coffee. It has become almost a universal truism that cops go to stores and shops and fast food places and drag their sacks. Free coffee here, free soda water there, free cookies from this place, a hamburger here or there and on and on. Now Souryel could really wind your stem over the question of ethics and accepting and expecting the provision of such liberties was often his starting point and most police do not like to discuss this, or to have anyone tell them that it is unethical. To many it will seem like a big to do about nothing. Yet, as most criminologist and psychologist who really understand the profession will state, the taking or accepting of little things, that to most will appear of no consequence, is in fact the building blocks which lead to other and more serious ethical misconduct. In Brownwood, just for an example, as their have been many witnessed, was an officer who exercised such gross unethical conduct in the pursuit of freebies that it caused a seriously unfavorable state of mind with at least one merchant and businessman. The owner of a fast food establishment wanted to show his support of the police. So, on a given day at lunch an officer that was on duty and in uniform could come to his place of business and receive a free hamburger, fries and drink. This particular officer whose girth indicated that he had never missed a meal, took the offer literally. On each such day, whether he was on duty or not, the portly officer would go home, put on his uniform, get his wife and kids and go to the establishment. There he would obtain food for the whole brood and himself, for free. This went on for months and months and the owner was astounded, but did not know how to reign in the wanton abuse of his good nature. Finally, out of disgust for the continued sack dragging and abuse of a privilege by one officer, the owner discontinued the allowance. Those other officers who accepted from time to time were thus turned away in the future. The owner who liked to have the police presence in his establishment lost out also. Yet, one officer, whose unethical abuse of a good natured and well meaning businessman, not to mention the uniform he wore and the oath he took, turned this business owner against the police. All for personal gain of some damn hamburger and fries. It was, or could never be, worth the disgrace and humiliation to the profession. There can be no excuse for an officer to ever use his or her badge to secure any personal gain. Soruyel also disagreed with this practice and stated so very eloquently and convincingly. In the years to come, as Chief of Police, the acceptance of gratuities, which were already covered in the statutes of the State of Texas, would be incorporated in the no no section of the police department regulations that I wrote and installed. Not to the pleasure of those who they were aimed at, if you preach ethics, you have to have ethical conduct and leadership as an example for others to follow. To only talk about something does no good without demonstration.

So we have seen how there are those who believe that to protect their positions they must be in "control" of everything that might affect their position. The number of examples of this type of mentality are astronomical. The other factor that was mentioned was professional jealousy. This is mainly a state of mind held by an individual whose own skills are abilities are less than those of another, but the individual takes it as a personal insult if the other individual can perform and achieve at a higher degree. The individual who is possessed of this malady cannot fathom that he or she needs to hone their own skills, they can only seek to tear down the other person.

In the following example of true life stupidity and corruption we will see how such a defect of common sense can be injurious to not only the profession, but also to the people we are suppose to serve. Now, it has to be said that religious figures, of whatever stripe, are not all pure as driven snow. In fact, some are real snakes in the grass. Does anyone need to be reminded of Jim Baker, to mention only one. About a month before school let out for the summer, a young girl's body was found on a lonely country road south of Brownwood. I was in my office listening to the radio traffic on a scanner when he became apparent that the county had another homicide on its hands. I telephone the DA and he came over and we listened to the cross talk of the Sheriff office with dispatch and the various Deputies that were on the scene. Now the DA had tried to assure that in such cases our office was immediately notified so that we could assist in the investigation and also prepare any actions that would be required. This is not an unusual arrangement. Yet, the Sheriff knew better and no call came. Finally, Fred said lets go and we drove out to the scene to get a first hand feel for the situation. They might as well have sold tickets and employed jugglers. It was a circus to say the least. There was no crime scene protection. The few pictures taken were meaningless. There was no thorough examination of the area of the crime and so on and so on. We were able to keep up with most of the actions of the SO as the PD got involved since the girl lived in town and went to school there also. It came to pass that the girl was being "counseled" by her preacher and he was a fairly far out non-denominational type of dubious intent and history. After a long period of time passed and there was no progress, even though the pastor and wife were suspects, the DA called a meeting of everyone to try and put some order to the situation. The effort basically failed. Not because Fred was on the wrong track, but because the PD and the SO personnel were at odds with each other and the Sheriff and the Chief were both of the same attitude, we know best.

At that point, the DA advised me to do whatever I could to discover the truth and he was not concerned with the potential for anyone not liking what would come of that effort. Thus a background investigation was commenced, on the preacher. I found an ex-wife in Illinois and brother, did things get interesting. After talking to this former spouse for two hours long distance, I filled the DA in. The preacher had a history of sexually forcing himself on young girls. The victims all looked pretty much the same. The profile developed, even matched his own daughter from the previous marriage. We had struck pay dirt where no one else had been willing to look. Another meeting was called and the parties arrived with the same opinion, they would handle it and did not care to participate in any avenue of investigation developed by the DA. Okay, don't Fred replied, but I am sending my investigator to Illinois to develop all the information possible. Once they realized that the die was cast and it would happen without them, they were afraid of not being there in case something did come of it. So, now two teams would go. A PD detective would go with me and the Texas Ranger would go with the SO Investigator. Almost two weeks later I got back to Brownwood with a bucket load of information. The preacher was the target, but there was a fly in the ointment. The SO had interviewed the preacher and wife several times. Or I should say, they had talked to them several times, to no avail. In fact, the SO gave them a polygraph test, but failed to ask the appropriate questions in a manner consistent with good and acceptable procedures. In addition, due to, shall we say warnings provided to the suspects, the preacher would not talk the DA's office. There had been so many mistakes made in the investigation and the level of cooperation was so low that it was quickly achieving the status of non-solvable. To make a long story short, stupidity, jealousy, incompetence and a total unwillingness to get along were the causes of a murder suspect getting away with sexually abusing a young child and then in shooting that young child to death. Years later, when interviewing for another position I was ask what one thing I regretted most. My answer was that I regretted not getting right in the middle of the case from the beginning. The police officials cared less for the victim of a dirty crime, than they did for themselves and their putrid reputations. As far as I am concerned that is corruption.

The disability of professional jealousy and its moribund impact upon law enforcement officials in Brown County did not end there. Neither had it started there. The sad part is, no matter what you do, who you are, how much you try to get along and cooperate, you cannot completed sever the ugly head of jealousy and stupidity. Many times when I have interviewed with prospective employers I have been ask, "what is your biggest weakness?". Invariably, telling the truth is not always the best policy, but I have replied, "I lack patience with incompetence and stupidity". That is the truth, but telling the truth is not necessarily the way to win a job. However, I have looked at this way. Police officers, of any type of agency, hold a power over others unequaled in our world. The actual power of life and death, freedom versus imprisonment and much more. Officers must attend and successfully complete a long basic training program. Many have more than a high school education. All are required to attend regular inservice training to be updated on laws, procedures and tactics, so they are not the run of the mill yuk that you can meet on the street. They are suppose to be educated, trained, honorable, honest and protectors of the constitution, laws and citizens of this land. So, I don't feel I am being rigid in my position that bad cops have no place in my profession.

The brutal attack, long running abuse and the finality of the gunshot to the head of the little girl would remain with me for a long time. It was not the last such boondoggle of a case to take place in Brown County. In the early summer one year the DA office got wind of the fact that the wife of a director of one of our banks had been kidnapped and a ransom had been demanded. Steve called me and got me up to speed and the hunt was on. We called in the FBI from Abilene to get more manpower and some legal leverage. The ransom call was to come in to a pay phone at the Dairy Queen in Goldthwaite. The Sheriff had sent his people out checking roads and doing nothing terribly constructive. The Sheriff went to check something and the Texas Ranger got in a plane and was flying around. Now, if there had been leads to run, that would have all been fine, but to wonder around without any true direction was wasting time. The bodywire belonging to DPS was in the office, but the Ranger was gone. The FBI agents were standing around waiting. I was waiting. Miraculously, the lady got loose from the abandoned house, that she had been left in and had found her way to a road and then back to town. The ransom call was still on as the kidnappers did not know she had gotten loose. Finally, Tom Clark, Mike Morris and I decided we couldn't wait any longer, so I picked up the body wire and we left to meet with the husband of the victim and be there when the call came in . I wired the husband, we put together a plan and off we went. At the Dairy Queen we waited, no call. At closing time, we had to shut it down. It was 9 pm. We got back to Brownwood and discussed the situation and everyone started to head home. What the crooks did not know was the Dairy Queen closed before they planned to make their call. So just after midnight, before I got home, they called the victims house again and stated that the next call would come in at a pay phone by a BBQ place north of Austin would come in shortly. The Sheriff, in all his expertise, had pulled the plug on the trace we had working, so we could not discern where the call came from, but we raced to the designated intersection and waited. There was another problem. The crooks did not know that the next chosen pay phone was out of order. Way up in the early morning we got back to Brownwood and later learned that a meet had been called in to the residence for a location in north Austin. The Sheriff did not bother to tell us. He called Austin and told them. Well, we found out later that the surveillance on the money delivery was choked before the pickup crook could make contact with his buddies. The only good point was that the pickup crook got nabbed and was hauled back to Brownwood, but he was not talking. So, the identity of the others was only speculation.

This situation continued for a few weeks and the SO was getting absolutely no where. Then one afternoon, a young woman who had been coming to see the crook in jail, visited again. She was driving a racy

Porsche and instinct was saying she knew more than she was telling or she was directly involved. A PD officer and a Deputy and I talked and we decided to tail her to see where she went and who she met. Now this broad was not dumb and spotted the PD unit and the race was on. She did some zigs and zags and then headed east out of town toward Comanche. She had not seen me, but by the time I hit the east limit of Early, the damnedest hail storm hit that I had ever seen. I mean it was flat coming down and made driving almost impossible, but I knew she was ahead of me and I felt there was more to this than met the eye, so I stuck with it. I radioed ahead and ask Comanche to watch for the car and tell me which way she went. Between the hailstones and the speed I was driving it was interesting to say the least. Comanche advised she was headed through to toward Stephenville, so I kept on moving and finally, the hail let up and my foot pressed the pedal even more. She was running hard and thought she had out run anyone that may be trying to follow her, but the radio is quicker than greased lightning. With a little help from officers up the road I knew where she was and I was gaining. By the time I got close enough to see her in the distance, she had relaxed her vigil and pulled in to a motel. I took up a surveillance position and waited. She went in to a room and the time dragged by. After a while a male came out of the room and put some things in the car. It was the man who had formally worked at the victims ranch and was believed to be the ringleader. Bingo!! I radioed back to Brownwood and requested the Ranger or others to come give me a hand as a rolling surveillance is a dicey situation to begin with, but with only one car to do the work, the odds were against me. The reply was, we don't believe it is worth it. Okay. So, I called to Stephenville and finally got some help from that Ranger and unlike some of his compadres, he knew what he was doing. We cut it up as we drove, because the suspects had gotten in their fast moving machine and headed east. At Hico, an officer told us which way they turned, toward Waco. In Waco, we were joined by DPS intelligence agents and headed for Austin. Close to Austin the intel boys, with whom I could not communicate, got spotted and the race was on.

The Ranger and I pulled in to a motel parking lot on IH-35 and discussed the mess as we were both out in the cold on local whereabouts of anyone. Then, as if by a miracle, the crooks in their Porsche, pulled up right in front of us. There was not tail on them. The guy went in as if to get a room, but came out shortly and left. The tail was on again as we advised the dispatcher and we headed to the south side of Austin. Without them becoming aware of our presence, they stopped at a high rise motel and checked in, got their bags and rode th elevator up to their designated floor. We were right there with them.

I got myself a room and called the DA to let him know what all had transpired. He was wondering where I was as he could not find me. By the time I had explained the rolling surveillance and the Brownwood boys response to the call for assistance, he was not in a good mood. The surveillance continued for days while the DA worked to put together every scrap of information we collected in to a warrant that would meet muster in the court. Over the long haul, we bagged the racing woman and the ringleader and they all were convicted. Through the determination and gut hunch of the DA Investigator the log jam had been broken, with the very able assistance of officers in several other cities and counties. However, the Brown County SO again had egg on its face from being uncooperative and imcompetent. Now, before I forget, the main protagonist of this debilitating attitude was the Sheriff himself. There were men in the department that were good and would work with anyone, but not at the risk of losing their jobs. The professional jealousy continued to rule, and only got worse.

On December 1, 1992 I arrived in Hereford, Texas with my clothes in a travel trailer, pulled by my rusting pickup truck. That first night in the flatness of Texas was an experience in itself. During the night I woke up with icicles in my hair and shivering uncontrollably. My propane tanks had run out fuel for the heater and it was about fifteen below zero. Welcome to the Panhandle.

The next morning, it was off to work in new territory and to meet new people. It was to be a few good years. The boss is Roland Saul. Roland is a very tall and strapping man of unquestioned integrity. He had two assistant district attorneys and two secretaries. The District Judge is David Wesley Gulley, another quality individual. To the north, in the next county, was the County Attorney, special District Attorney, Don Davis. In the years to come we all worked closely together and enjoyed a lot of success. Yet, in that first month, my inquisitiveness and investigative knowledge would lead to a difficulty. Granted, I made the situation by my investigation, but I did not make the animosity that would follow.

It is appropriate at this point to discuss another aspect of the police profession and that is professional jealousy or professional mistrust. They are generally different, but they can also be the same or at least molded in to the same situation. For example, the FBI and the CIA rarely work together, even on the same subject. The FBI and the DEA do get along like they should. The FBI does not trust many local law enforcement agencies or personnel. Most local law enforcement agencies and personnel don't trust the FBI. We have heard many times from the DEA at TNOA meetings that we are here to help you. Right. Only trouble is that help is rare in coming and nearly always has strings attached. The FBI rarely shares information with locals and at times not even with other Federal agencies. Why? Trust? Maybe at times, in various situations, such a position is understandable, especially when locals officers are in the middle of situations involving corruption and are taking no local action. Having been a Federal agent I have seen many situations where the locals could not be trusted. Yet, I have also seen agents from Federal agencies that also could not be trusted. Trust has to be earned. There is no doubt about that, but to assume that no one can be trusted except ourselves is also a dangerous attitude. It is also a situation that will not hold up to scrutiny. Then there is the jealousy of one agency or officer for another. Based on the accomplishments of one the other takes umbrage, even when it is totally uncalled for. So the other convinces himself that there must be limits installed or impediments erected to lessen the positive impact of the other and before you know it the situation has grown like a snowball rolling down hill. Unable to stop it, with countering actions from the other, it grows to an almost out of control condition. From that point it becomes extremely difficult to reverse or correct. Did you make someone else look bad? Do you have the capability to make someone else look bad? Is there a personal dislike which fuels the animosity? Do you dislike the success of another in your own back yard or in an area where you believe you are the top banana? On and on it can go with the reasons being limitless. Thus, officers, agents, agencies can undertake attitudes and actions that under-cut others, not for any good and descent reason, but for the stupidity of the person who is initiating the attitude or action.

Towards the end of December of 1992 I was in the office in Hereford and basically bored due to not having anything to work on. It was a quiet time, with Christmas approaching and snow covering almost everything. I went in and ask Roland if he had anything that needed to be worked on and he did not. He did suggest that I could look at a box of old files if I wanted to. It was something to do. So over the next couple of days, I went through some old, very old, and dusty files of cases that never went any-where. Then, as if a present, I found one file that caught my attention.

One of the lessons I learned early on and had reinforced on numerous occasions, is that you do not discount anything, out of personal conven-ience, or because you just do not want to, or the person it is coming from seems to be a looney tune or any other so called reason. Way too many investigators leave there common sense in the bathroom with their shav-ing gear. Others only look upon what they do as a pay check and believe if it is not "assigned" or "out of the time frame they work", don't bother me. Really a poor attitude and proof is as abundant as feathers on a goose.

After reading the case file of the eighteen month old baby dying, I read it again. And then again. This was no ordinary death. My gut and experi-ence told me this baby was murdered. In fact, it was a type of murder that most of my peers did not know about or if they did, understand. Not even the medical and criminal justice system really knew of it and understood it. Yet, I knew the baby had been killed, not necessarily intentionally, but killed nevertheless. The deed was committed coldly and with total disregard for the baby. The death came at the hands of the mother. It was Muchausens Syndrome by Proxy, or I was the tooth fairy. Convinced of what I had found, I went in and ran it down to Roland and his first assistant, Jim English. They had heard of the malady, but were far from convinced, yet Roland was smart enough to recognize the potential and acknowledged my background in the subject. The word was go, just be careful. So, for the next three months I talked to dozens of witnesses, drove thousands of miles, read and cross checked thousands of documents, stirred up the Reid family to no end, and perked up the attention of the prosecutor in Iowa.

It all came together. Tanya Reid had killed her baby. Tanya Reid had been regularly, repeatedly, heartlessly abusing her children for years. Iowa almost tagged her for the near death of her son. The Texas case would not be almost. March of 1993 crept up on us, the grand jury was scheduled to meet and I had put together a battery of details, facts and associated information that would show anyone what took place. Tanya Reid was indicted for Murder. It may seem like the hard part was over, but far from it. Now came the task of putting together the witnesses, the evidence and the circumstances to show a petit jury and the court what had taken place. Then you have to also contend with the "experts" who wouldn't admit that day is day unless they were paid to say so. I couldn't believe some of the dribble that medical doctors, who are suppose to be so damn smart, came out with. Not to mention the lawyers, but you can excuse some of their antics as they are paid to do whatever to save their client. Roland and Jim English were definitely no dummies. Roland had been in the county for a long time and knew the people. Jim had an eagles eye and an elephants memory for digging out the legal maneuvers that would be required to sustain a conviction. The battle was engaged. After months of preparation. The obtaining of and movement of dozens of out of state witnesses, the jury came back with the verdict. Guilty!! In an interview with the Amarillo television station, I was ask why did I spend so much time on something that had taken place ten years ago. My reply was, someone had to speak for the baby, it was that simple. Greg Olsen, a writer of some repute, got wind of the case early on and came to Hereford and watched the whole thing. He wrote a book about Reid and the entire situation entitled *Mockingbird*. It is a damn good read.

Now you are probably wondering, why in the hell did I go in to this as it has nothing to do with the main thrust of this work? Well, if you are thinking that, you are wrong. Shortly, after Reid was indicted, the current Chief of Police in Hereford telephoned me at my office. Now the Chief had been the immediate past investigator for the DA. Anyway, he wanted to know who gave the Reid case to me, how did I get it? I told him I found it in a box of closed, but unsolved situations in the office. He wanted to know why his department did not have it and why I did not call him. Needless to say, Chiefee was upset. He was catching some heat about why the PD did not know about this, since it took place within the city limits. My only, and admittedly somewhat sarcastic reply was, you were the investigator here and the case was in this office and you did not do anything with it, so don't complain to me. Well, that did not go down to well, but I did not give a big rat's rear. From that day forward, we were speaking, but less than professionally close. Because of his attitude it did make getting work done, at various time, a little more difficult.

Professional competence admittedly has to be acquired. How? Through training, through personal commitment, through dedication to achievement, with a desire to be the best, and with deep experience involvement. If you only do what you have to. If you only slide through and or by. If it is only a pay check. If it is "don't bother with that" mentality. If you want everything handed to you instead of earned. You will not be professionally competent, much less become a recognized expert for what you do know and do. That is the exact situation that over fifty percent of all the law enforcement personnel in the United States are wrapped up in. At the risk of being brash, I rank in the top ten percent in the State of Texas and the top twenty percent in the United States. I am damn proud of that as I have worked damn hard to achieve and learn and to be one of the best. The Reid case was a national story. It has a book written about it. The District Attorney was quoted widely. We, as a team, had done a damn good job. We earned our pay and we earned respect. It felt good, but this is only a slight indication of the professional conflicts to come.

Overall the PD and the Sheriff's department were made of up of pretty good people. Most of them cared, but through no direct faults of their own, were limited. Three subsequent investigations were to reveal the underlying attitudes. One was a double murder in Vega at a truck stop. The County Attorney, Don Davis, called me in and Roland agreed.

Now Vega, Texas is only a wide spot in the road on IH-40, west of Amarillo. It is wind swept, isolated and in the winter, cold as a well diggers foot in Montana. At the scene, one male deceased was on the ground out by the fuel pumps. The female clerk, also deceased, was in the back storage room. No one could provide any cogent idea or clue. Someone had walked in the blood on the floor, but would not own up to it. There were no other witnesses known. All the time, the breaker was right there in front of everyone. A plastic cold drink container, full, unopened, and still sweating, was on the counter. It was taken to the lab in Amarillo and printed. Bingo. The prints matched an escapee from the east coast. The hunt was on and it went west in to New Mexico, Arizona, California and finally back in to Nevada. Unfortunately, we could not nail him, before he killed a Nevada State Trooper and was later captured in the desert north and east of Reno. Traveling to Carson City to meet with the investigators for the State of Nevada, I wound up leading the interrogation and obtained a confession. All of this did not exactly sit well with the Sheriff there, and while David is a good man, he did not have the skills, but he got irritated and over nothing but professional jealousy. I worked very closely with his deputy and Don Davis so there was no true reason for the irritation, but it existed.

Another case in the same county came from the death of an elderly lady in a motel room. The only other person present was her husband. Davis wanted my input. Now this case was a mess. No evidence was collected and or preserved to speak of. The Justice of Peace had decided there was no case as it was suicide. Few photographs remained. Yet, in the examination of what was in existence and with some background investigation, I should the County Attorney why it was murder. The husband was tired of taking care of his spouse, wanted what little money there was and so he came to Vega. Slit her wrist, made a show of cutting his own, and let her bleed to death. The tell in the case was he had moved the body of his wife on the bed, before calling the police, but after she was dead. From that point on, his story went to mush. Indicted for murder, he was convicted. It embarrassed the Sheriff's office some, the JP a whole bunch, and here we went again. The question has been ask of me, why do you do such investigations when you know it is going to cause a problem. My reply is, do I let criminals, especially murder suspects, get away with their crimes, just because those who could not do it right to begin with, get mad when I do it right. Obviously, the answer is no. In addition, I freely admit to not having ever performed in what is known in todays world as "politically correct". If you are paid to do the job, do it. If you can't do it, say so and get someone who can. Then you learn from them and the next time, you do it. Of course, I would be lying through my teeth if I did not admit to being self-gratified by the results of my work. Especially after others had failed, but refused to admit they had failed.

Now this next example will be in a little more detail and it should amaze you at the incompetence and "politically correct" mentalities that guided the work. Yep, it generated heat, but the murderer and murderess went to prison.

Roland Saul, like other District Attorney's, wanted his investigator called out on the worst crimes. So it was that about 2:30 am, awakened from a fast sleep, the Sheriff's office called about a death case. It was so far out in the sticks the county had to pipe sunlight there. Of course, if you

have ever been in the Panhandle, most of the land and settlers, are that
same way. When I got the farm house in far northern Deaf Smith County,
there were several Deputies and a Texas Ranger sitting there in the living
room batting the breeze. The male victim had been taken to the hospital.
The crime scene was not protected. No evidence had been collected. The
wife of the victim had gone to the hospital. The young guy who lived with
them, was not around and his location was not known. The story
imparted to me was nothing short of amazing. The victim comes home. Is
standing in the kitchen. Is shot in the head by an unknown assailant, from
the outside and through a screened window. The wife was taking a shower
and did not know what happened. End of story. Horse Apples. I looked
around and found more holes in the story than you would find in a
woolen closet full of moths. First, the shower tub was not even damp. The
shower curtain was not even damp. The bar of soap, top and bottom, were
stone dry. The soap dish was not damp. There was no damp towel or floor
towel. The wife supposedly heard the shot, at 1:30 AM, but was not concerned. Got out of the shower and put her clothes on. Put her clothes on.
Then she goes and finds her hubby. She calls 911 and reports it, but,
….well you would just have to listen to the call that was recorded.
Outside, on the ground was a big mortar brick, and the theory was that
the shooter stood on that brick and fired the shot through the window.
Where was the footprints? Where was the spent casing? How did the
shooter leave the area? What was the motive? Did the dogs bark? They
barked at everything or everyone else. Not a single other thing was disturbed or taken. It did not take a rocket scientist to figure out that there
was far more to this than the officers on the scene knew or were even trying to find out.

     Needless to say, the victim did not make it. Later that day I had the
opportunity to view the wife at the Sheriff's Office. It was a telling obser-
vation, at least to me. No tears, no emotion, nothing. Just matter of fact
and cold, going through the motions. By this time all of the family members had rallied round and were supporting the wife/mother. The SO had

arrested the eighteen year old boy who was living in the home with the victim and wife. He had given a "confession" and admitted to shooting the victim. When all the family, including the wife, came to the courthouse, I ask the Deputy/Investigator who was going to interview the wife if he was going to ask the hardball questions. His reply was what do you mean and I stated that there was good reason to believe that the stories just did not add up and that she may be involved. He replied that this was a sensitive situation politically and all and that "they were not going to go down that road". Well, there it was. Influence was about and they were not going to look for the facts. Later that day, Roland and I watched as the wife and her brood departed the courthouse. I told Roland then, there is more to this than we know right now. We discussed it and I informed him of all that I knew at that point in time. His reply was cautious, but searching. Roland told me to find out what I could, but to go at it easy. The hunt for the key was on. First, came an interview with the kid. There were more inconsistencies in his story than you could shake a stick at. There was a revelation that came from that interview that would later tie it all up in a big bow. Background work came next. We dug up every piece of information we could find from just about anyone who knew the farming couple and their family. In a couple weeks, in fact on the very day the Grand Jury was meeting to consider the case, I convinced the wife to come in for an interview. She laid it all on the kid. They had taken him in, gave him a home, and then he kills her husband. This interview was recorded and the poor wife laid the kid out to dry. Shortly thereafter, I got the kid upstairs and in front of a Deputy for a witness we undertook another interview. Only, this time, we played the tape recorded interview of the wife giving the kid up for the needle. It turns out, as I stated earlier, that there was a revelation that would tie it all up. Yep, this fiftish wife had been having a long running affair with the eighteen year old, that they treated as a son. What a mom! The kid saw the handwriting on the wall and volunteered the true story. The wife used the kid. She convinced him that if he killed her husband, the farm and all they possessed would be his, including the wife.

They had sex during this conversation and needless to say, the kid was not thinking with the right part of his anatomy. The wife, before the interview with the kid concluded, was an active partner in the murder. I got the wife back in and we went at it, politely, even deviously, for over two hours. She was sharp, quick on her feet, and determined not to get caught up in a bad story. Yet, I was no virgin to this type of work either. I knew she was in it up to her sagging bosoms, but I needed her to say something that would prove her culpability. That is where the questioning got down right sneaky. Before it was all over, the wife made a slip and stated she knew about the plan to kill her husband, but then quickly realized she had messed up and went off in another direction. I took all the information down to the Grand Jury and gave it to Roland. We conducted a hand full of further interviews and went over the scene and financial records, but dear wife got indicted. The family was livid, wife's attorney was expectedly condemning and the public, well, they were not sure. As for the SO, well, they got irritated to say the least. Why? Only slightly, because of the wife's involvement, but more so because the DA Investigator had made them look bad. Tough! If all you are in this profession for is the paycheck and not to uphold your oath, get the hell out. If you don't know how to do something, ask? Go to training. Watch, look, and listen — learn!! Don't blame me for your incompetence and stupidity. Wife was convicted. Kid testified against her. The evidence built was powerful and she still sits in prison. She got the husband "off of my stomach", but the results were not those anticipated.

The ten years I spent working for four District Attorneys, all damn good men by the way, were the best of my career. I was allowed to do what I wanted, within reason of course, to run with precious little information in seeking a criminal, and was regularly called on to handle situations that no one else wanted to, knew how to, or gave a damn about. I made some enemies to say the least. I also won respect. When I first started in 1967, I had a sergeant tell me, if you don't make anyone mad, you aren't doing your job. Conversely, if you do your job, you are going to make people mad. Oh how true.

Before leaving the District Attorneys Office in Hereford there was to be one more major and long running situation that would add to the locals animosity. Like most cities, Hereford had a narcotics problem. Everyone talked a good game about catching the dopers, even the Task Force agent who was stationed there, but very little was getting done. Now, it doesn't take a Rhodes Scholar intellect to catch a doper. Most of them are dumber than two boxes of rocks or they wouldn't be on the damn stuff to begin with. So, after talking to Roland, and getting a little money, we purchased a body wire and got with the program. Everyone that got tagged for possession was a potential source of assistance. Slowly, we built up a few "spies" and started making buys from dealers. Each transaction was recorded and sometimes we got to take photographs. The effort began to grow, and grow, and before you knew it, everyone wanted in. They could see what was coming and did not want to be left out of the glory. Well, in that city as in others, you have to play it close to the vest, so we controlled the information and access to it, and who was permitted to participate. The last, for that particular series, effort came when we took down probably the biggest cocaine supplier in the County. Had him on tape making the sale, and then tagged him with a search warrant and seized tens of thousands of dollars, over a pound of cocaine and assorted other stuff. As cases go, it was not big, and was not the biggest that I had ever made, but it was a good wake up call for the citizens who knew it was there, but did not know how bad it was. It was also a lesson for those who were suppose to be doing something. Doing something was not that damn hard. Fifty odd dope dealers were caught in the act, some from prominent families, and it sure slowed down the trade, at least for a while.

Now, as I said, this duty was great. Making cases, busting crooks and helping those who can't and don't know how to help themselves. There was a lot of satisfaction that went with the job, but creditors did not think much of satisfaction or awards or honor or integrity. So, my wife and I decided that if we were to make the money we would like to I would have to try and find a decent city in which to become the Chief of Police. For several months, we read notices, researched cities and made application for Chief positions. The break, or so we though, was to come on the very day that the Oklahoma City bombing took place. The Mayor of Galena Park called me about meeting with him to discuss my becoming their new Chief. I was excited, nervous, and even skeptical. My wife and I were treated superbly, at city expense. We talked to everyone we could trying to find out what we were not being told by the city. It looked good. In fact, upon reflection, it looked to good to be true. And, went it isn't, it isn't. What was to come would be lesson and a half and not soon forgotten. While I have intentionally set about to work in all the corners of this vast profession, in retrospect, I truly miss this ten years, the success, even the failures, and the peace of mind that went with doing a damn good job.

"I will do anything to win."

Al Gore
Vice President of the United States

CHAPTER SIX

LOSING IS NOT AN OPTION

Your high school football team, or your college alma mater team loses to your high profile rivalry on homecoming night or on that traditional weekend of the year. Sure, it is hard to accept, and you don't like it, but it is only a game. You don't engage in conduct, which would harm another, just to win. Or do you? History is replete with incidents of this type being manipulated by others. Gamblers, rich alumni or some other misguided soul. The competitive spirit is in most of us, at least, at one time or another, and is something that no one should discourage. It can be positively directed, productive and beneficial to all concerned. Yet, there are some more ugly aspects, which seem to dominate the competitive spirit and resulting actions.

Admittedly, I love catching criminals. I make no bones about it. I have spent all of my adult life learning, training and, in a sense practicing, that tradecraft on every case I came in contact with. I also like to win. We all like to win. We all like to be recognized, honored, touted and bestowed with garlands of well wishes, but at what price, if any. Will I do anything

to catch a criminal. No. I will do anything that is within the law and the
code of criminal procedure and the rules of evidence and the penal code,
but not *anything*. I have never sandbagged an individual. I have caught
over two thousand felons, and each one was caught fair and square.
However, there are those who will do anything to win. And I do mean
anything.

There are rules in just about every human endeavor. Even the scumbag
dopers have rules. Not very good ones admittedly, but they have rules.
Team sports have rules. The law has rules. Even in politics there are rules.
You may not recognize them as rules, but that is what they are suppose to
be. The exact number of incidents will never be known, but law enforcement agencies, on all levels, and far too many law enforcement officers, on
all levels, believe and have demonstrated that losing is not an option with
them. So, they commit perjury, falsify evidence, engage in illegal conduct,
withhold information and actually commit crimes. The most recent and
notorious evidence of this mentality comes to us from the City of Angels.
Los Angles has touted the professionalism and effectiveness of its police
department for eons of time. Yet, the Rampart Division was home to a
large group of officers who were so intent on relieving the city of the gang
problem and narcotics that they falsified evidence, gave perjured testimony, wrote false reports, laid evidence of criminality on individuals they
wanted convicted and imprisoned, and in general totally disgraced themselves, the department and the profession, at will. We aren't talking about
a few cases of wrongful imprisonment or conviction, but rather, hundreds.
I recently watched an interview with one Sergeant from that division,
under whom some of these officers served. This Sergeant was orally and
physically upset that the department and his division were being painted
as corrupt. He was upset that any of his personnel would be suspended
and accused of criminal misconduct. Yet, he never said anything negative
about the officers and their misdeeds. On top of that, he made the comment that he did not know of anything like the charges being leveled was
going on. He did not know? Or, he did not want to know? Or, he knew

about the dung being spread, but wouldn't say anything even if he had a mouthful? This is not the kind of individuals that should be in our profession. Any officer involved in that type of conduct is no better than the ones they are attempting to set up. In fact, they are worse.

Whether, the badge is from the LAPD, NOPD, FBI, INS, NYPD, or any other agency, such deliberate conduct is unforgivable. Trying to catch and convict Wen Ho Lee of Los Alamos infamy, was a just and good cause. Anyone who sells or provides national security secrets to our enemies, which China actually is, is someone who should be legally drawn and quartered. Yet, the counter-intelligence efforts and investigative efforts were short of the mark and less than timely. So, an agent falsely testifies, giving the court the impression that evidence exists that in fact did not exist. This is another example of winning at any cost, and is wrong, wrong and more wrong. Now no one should labor under the illusion that corruption exists only within the law enforcement profession. Not hardly. In fact, at a point in time not to distance from the present, I recall reading a breakdown of the occupations of those individuals who were incarcerated within the penal system of this country. Care to take a guess about which profession led the way? Cops? No, it was Attorneys. They spend all that time in school and then in the law library and in the courthouse and they get to believe that only they know the law. Assuming the mantel of omnipotence, they come to venture in to areas and activities that they know are illegal, but then they are so damn smart, they can work it so no one will ever catch them. Right? Wrong!

All across this nation and in most nations that I am aware of, police engage in the time worn tradition of not saying anything about what another officer may be doing that is not up to the mark. The code of silence is strong—and misdirected. The same is true with attorneys, doctors, engineers, judges, politicians and many other professions. You aren't suppose to turn on your own kind. That is quietly and indirectly instilled in rookies of all working venues. If a police officer observes a fellow officer committing a criminal act, it is his or her duty to report it, but what happens if they do report it? They are shunned, berated, ostracized and even placed in harms way, without backup. Sooner or later they will be run out of the agency in which they serve. Trying to obtain a position after that becomes even more difficult as individuals take it upon themselves to poison the well of information with the potential new agency. I know this from first hand experience. So, the question arises, is it worth it? Is it worth the heartache, loss of income, harm to family, threats, and so much more, to do your duty and enforce the law, no matter who or what? That is a decision that each individual has to make, but the over riding answer is yes. Once you give in to the pressures of silence in light of criminality you are co-opted and will slowly be dragged down and into more and more misconduct and illegal deeds. Your silence is used against you as a threat in the future. It is a vicious circle and can lead to no good end. What is funny, in a sense, is that here are men and women who all carry firearms, most know how to use them, most are given good training in survival and tactics, they regularly go up against armed felons and individuals who will take their lives at the drop of a hat, and they do it daily. Scared, probably, each time it happens, but 99% make it through, only to be turned in to jelly by a police officer making threats to keep quiet about police corruption. Ironic.

Within most agencies there is a support structure for officers and agents who become involved with alcohol or narcotics, are involved in a deadly force useage incident, or have some traumatic event hit them within the family. Yet, for all the ethics training that is mandated, for all the rhetoric that is spewed forth, for all the regulations and policies that are written, there is not one single avenue of support provided to any officer, that I am aware of, who does the right thing and turns in corrupt officers. You can even go out here, within the past ten years, and use cocaine or any other drug, or you can be convicted of a crime, and as in Seattle and other states and cities, you can be employed as a police officer. Where did this insanity come from? Is our nation so screwed up, money driven, and short of quality individuals that we have to hire dope heads to be police officers and supposedly protect society from other dope heads and criminals?

As this work is being written our nation is witnessing a somewhat tawdry example of history being made by politicians and those who would be politicians. The 2000 election was held on November 7, to elect a President and Vice President of the United States, along with a myriad of other lesser officials. For the past eight years we have also witnessed some of the most shameful conduct by the occupier of the White House that has existed in this century. No, I do not forget President Nixon and the Watergate mess. I was involved in that case and the participants deserved everything they got and more. Yet, this more current long running situation is an example of the moral malaise that has attacked the very fabric of our nation. It is best classified as winning at any cost, or, losing is not an option. Clinton and a list of his cronies have been involved in obstruction of justice, perjury, manipulation of evidence, defiance of the law in general, and believing that the American people are so damn stupid and self-centered that they won't care what happens. Now comes Clintons protégé, Al Gore, who would be President, and further demonstrates that, as he himself stated, "will do anything to win". I will be the first to state that George W. Bush is not the sharpest tool in the box, but he cannot begin to heft the baggage that Gore brings with him and indirectly that provided by the Clinton and Gore administration. Granted, fifty million citizens voted for Gore. Another fifty million voted for Bush. True, both men, and their parties, are pulling out the "lets go to court cards" and trying to utilize the public relations antics of the down trodden to sway public opinion, but how far should anyone go—to win? I have long held a disgust for crooked cops and have never had a very high opinion for most politicians, but with the current election mess and the rising tide of public corruption, both in and out of the police profession ranks, my distaste is growing.

A similar mindset exists among members of many professions. A sharp example is the legal profession. There is hardly a week that goes by that one attorney or another is not busted or at least accused of illegal conduct. In fact, the legal profession as a whole is taking direct hits for its activities. A young and still idealistic attorney in Brownsville probably has made the

most cogent statement about the "system" of our laws and courts. Arnold
stated, in reply to a question about what happened to telling the truth and
finding the truth in court, that "truth, facts and justice are not the main
consideration in our system. The main focus is on winning and money".
The idea being that the more an attorney wins, the more money he gets,
the more cases that he gets, the more he wins and thus the more money he
gets. So the goal is to do whatever it takes to win. Losing, again, is not an
option. It has become chic to lie, cheat, steal, suborn, manipulate,
obstruct, misdirect, to play semantical games with the legal language or
even the most elementary understanding of what the word "is" is. I am
convinced that since the mid-1960's and the tragedy and triumphs surrounding the Vietnam War, that our nation, most particularly, the generations which came of age in that time, and since, has been steadily losing
any sense of direction when it comes to honor, duty, country, integrity,
ethics, morals, right and wrong and so many other principles that have
been the underpinning of our success for two hundred years. We are
becoming a nation more closely resembling a socialistic state than the
Great Republic. Engaging in any type of "game" where one or more people pit themselves against another or group is a normal human function
and whether the game involves muscle, words, ideas, or actions, those
games will continue. Yet, there has to be limits beyond which we will not
transgress. I don't recall who said it, but winning is not everything and the
end does not justify the means. We are on a slippery and increasingly steep
slope, headed in to an abyss of the unknown, and unless we move to correct this degradation, we, as a society and as the titular model for the
world, will not long prevail. There is always a cost. It may not come today,
tomorrow or even next year, but when it does come, can and will you be
able to afford it?

There can be no freedom without responsible living.

Thomas Jefferson

CHAPTER SEVEN

THE FRYING PAN

Have you ever tried to figure out what a "headhunter" or human resources or personnel type individual is looking for in a resume? I have arrived, after thousands of such exercises to gain employment, at the conclusion that there is no single or limited number of options by which your resume is to be constructed or for which it will contain and impart to another. It is everybody for themselves. When I crank out a resume I try to impart the achievement of training and experience, to divulge my capability to perform the task in question and to let the hiring party know that there is integrity and ethics in my conduct. In fact, I was contacted by an individual a short time ago that said he found my resume on Headhunters.net and the thing that jumped out at him was ethics. So I guess I have succeeded, if only in a limited way, in achieving the goals of imparting critical information. In the final analysis though, qualifications have absolutely nothing to do with employment. The controlling factors are race, political correctness, age, and the good old boy system. I had no grandiose dreams of being the Chief of Police in Houston or New York, but I did know that I had the skills and knowledge to be a good Chief, in any city. So when the mayor in Galena Park called, it was a ray of hope and a chance to achieve another of those dreams that many have as kids. True, the money would be nice too, but I saw distance horizons to be attained.

The preliminaries lasted over a several week period. The primary interview lasted about two hours. As usual, I gave them straight and unequivocal answers. In the end the job was mine and I left the DA's office, with some reluctance, but looked forward to new challenges. Brother, was it to be a challenge. From the mayor, a man who liked political involvement, but was basically honest, even though he was out of his depth in that game, came information about internal turmoil within the department. There was highly irregular, to say the least, activities by personnel while on duty, civil rights violations, missing or stolen evidence, and the ever present friction created by personnel against other personnel. Having seen these activities before, I was not put off at the prospect of having to deal with it. In fact the mayor told me that I was his number one choice from the beginning, because he saw integrity and the ability to solve problems. If he was shining me on, it worked. Not only was it true, but it was a salve to soothe the jitters of stepping off in a snake pit. What I did not know, is what the mayor did not tell me and that my wife and I had not uncovered. We came to the conclusion that Galena Park was a good city, led by good people, and while it had many problems, it was not a place that we would want to avoid living and working. So much for our foresight. Before I said yes, I met with the Acting Chief, who it would turn out, would be about the only person I could depend on. We went over the problems, the personnel, the budget, the operational structure and finally the political leanings. What became crystal clear was that the head of the internal problems was an individual who had been bounced from one agency to another for his conduct. A patrolman, affable, not overly intelligent, but not ignorant either, and an individual, I would learn, that would not hesitate to stoop to any level to achieve what he desired. Sounds like some current politicians we all know.

I agreed to accept the position, with high hopes and a directive from the mayor and council, to clean it up. That was straight and to the point, but in truth the road would have more twists and turns and potholes than Carter has pills.

What problems? We don't have any problems! Oh to have a nickel for every time I have heard that. At Galena Park, the list was long. A Sergeant, who utilized the services of a prostitute, in the patrol unit, while on duty. Cocaine use. Theft of items of property from the evidence room. Civil rights violations. Falsification of official records. There was even the cunning officer who would drive his patrol unit to a friends house, pull in the garage, close the door and go to sleep. Engaging in extra jobs was more important that your city job. Sure you could make more money, but doing an extra job while on duty was illegal as all hell. Of course there was the former Chief and Sergeant that would come to the station, check in on duty and then go board a bus with a bunch of others and be driven to Louisiana to gamble. Upon returning, he would go to the station, check out and go home. What kind of system was this? Now a lot of departments across the country have what are known as "reserve" officers. These are individuals who are trained and certified, but hold civilian positions and only want to work in law enforcement on a limited basis. This can be a great source of manpower and cost savings to any jurisdiction, if they are properly trained, supervised and administered. In Galena Park, there were seventeen full time personnel. The number of badges held by so called reserves exceeded thirty, and could easily have been more. Badges were handed out like candy and were political tokens to be redeemed at election time. Of course there are two other reasons that many want to be a reserve and that take precedence over the more mundane idea of serving. Those are, one the badge can get you out of things and in to other things. Two, for those without much self-esteem and purpose to their lives, it represents a symbol of status and power. One of the city councilmen held a reserve officers commission and that presented problems. The reserve unit, prior to my arrival, had been an almost autonomous entity. They did what they wanted when they wanted. Their "leader", and a very loose interpretation of that word to say the least, was a short, fat pharmacist whose personality was just short of that of a moldy piece of bread. His lack of knowledge about leadership and police work in particular was only exceeded by his vanity and quest for power. His quest for power would never really be achieved and his vanity was bolstered by the fact that he wore a rug... a hair piece to cover his dome. At the first meeting of the reserve officers, after my arrival, I attended, to take stock of those personnel and to provide them with a pep talk. The "Lieutenant of Reserves" had not gotten the hint. There was a new Chief in town and the old ways were not going to work. When he commented that this was "his" meeting, I retorted by looking at my badge and sarcastically said, "yep, that is what I thought, it says Chief of Police". There was a cold stare, a trembling lower lip, and grins from others, but he got the message. In a few weeks, he got another message, bye! So for the Chief or other administrator that thinks by having reserves he is getting something for nothing, alas, nothing is free. There is always a cost, of some kind.

The first problem that had to be fixed was the evidence room. There was no log of evidence and or property contained therein. No tags on many items. No reference to case numbers, dispositions or anything else. They didn't have the first damn clue about what to do, when, where or anything else. So I ordered a cage built and an inventory to be completed. Now, no Chief can do everything personally, but if you don't have anyone you can really trust, you better do it yourself. Well, the result was not unanticipated. After searching through records, reports, court documents and poor memories, it was found that guns were the primary items that were missing. Everyone of those with some degree of culpable exposure in this matter developed selective amnesia and we got no where, but it wouldn't happen any more, because the new system and the steel cage would see to that.

Then there was the setup of the Mayor's nephew. Now, I have seen some sneaky undertakings in my life, but this one was a little cut above, or is that below, some of the others. A patrolman, the anti-groups leader, was married. He also had a girlfriend who lived with him and his wife. Talk about broadminded. Ha! The officer was a dope head, but just smart enough to keep from getting caught. The game was to use the girlfriend to get next to the nephew, in the home of the nephew, which was also the home of the Mayor's sister, who was also the City Secretary. Confused? You should have been in my shoes. Anyway, on the pre-determined night, guess who shows up. The Houston PD and the Galena Park PD, with a search warrant. Found, was some dabbling amount of dope and the nephew was charged. The idiot Chief at the time, who took directions from the patrolman, went to the Mayor's house to inform him of the situation. The Mayor races over to find out what was going on. Outside the house is the patrolman, with a video camera, filming all of this. The patrolman verbally baits the Mayor, for recording of course. Also taken from the house, or rather we should say stolen from the house, by the patrolman and cohorts, was a photograph of the nephew and his girlfriend, naked, and doing what came natural. Was it evidence? No. Was it legal to take? No. Why then? Who knows, but they did. The only reason that makes any sense was for political embarrassment.

Now the Mayor wants answers. The Mayor relieves the idiot Chief. The next day, a copy of the video tape and all "pertinent" information mysteriously finds its way to the Television newsrooms and the print media. The Mayor is blasted, to say the least. Now, if you haven't figured it out, this was not a real dope bust. It was a bust of political embarrassment targeting the mayor. Pure and simple. Why? Well, the Mayor had beaten Mr. B for the job as Mayor. Mr. B was wanting back in and many supported him, including the patrolman and Chief, due to the, shall we say loosey goosey manner in which he allowed things to run. Not to mention, that the tenure of less than quality personnel would be continued under Mr. B and not under the new Mayor. Enter the new Chief—me. Illegalities within the police ranks were not going to be tolerated and EVERYONE knew it.

So, this lands on the Chief's desk by way of an official complaint. What a way to get a new job off the ground!

Have you ever been in one of those situations where you were screwed, blued and tattooed, no matter what you did? This was one of those. The investigation was conducted above board and there was no bias for either side, but in the end, the evidence was obvious. The civil service commission within the city was made up of three members. It turns out that two of them also supported Mr. B, so there was no action taken against the officer. The media in town, well it was definitely for Mr. B and there was a continuous barrage of venomous comments and untruths, but then that is the media. After nine months, enough was enough. It just wasn't worth it any more. Besides, it was obvious to many that the former Mayor would win the upcoming election and the former Mayor had already let it be known that all of the department heads would be fired and replaced. So why wait. I was out of there. With the election came the old Mayor. The department heads were fired. The old Chief became Chief again. The patrolman became Assistant Chief. The Assistant Chief ran the department and immediately fired or attempted to fire everyone in the department that had not lined up with him. His vengeful attitude towards me was to last for years. All that was wrong with the department did not get fixed in my short tenure, but we made a good run at it. Many of the reforms were cast out and the city and its department are once again a butt of jokes within the county. Yet, no effort is made, beyond mine, to fix the problems. THIS IS A CLASSIC EXAMPLE OF THE DICTUM, CITIZENS GET WHAT THEY WANT. It is not necessarily, a good thing.

Now, I freely admit that I have made my share of mistakes, both operationally and administratively. I made one, administratively, as Chief of Galena Park, which was blown completely out of proportion and for no reason other than "we have to get the Chief" and thus "we get the Mayor", or "if we get the Mayor, we get the Chief". After the evidence room was thoroughly reformed, there were seven handguns which were serviceable and the original owners could not be found. A part of the reformation job for the department was its image, to include the replacement of Houston PD look alike tin badges. The idea was to create a new and better image. Departments across the state and nation have often sold departmental weapons to officers. The court was requested to forfeit the seven in question here to the department. The mayor and council were approached about selling the weapons to the officers at reasonable prices, to place the funds in the general fund of the city, and then to utilize those funds to purchase the new badges for the department. Now, before I forget, this was a tough way to buy new badges, but the city did not have any money and the meager departmental budget was already in the red before I took over. I called the DA and the ATF to make damn sure the action intended was legal, and was told by both that it was. So, the mayor and council agreed, and any officer wishing to purchase a weapon was allowed to do so. The money went in to the city coffers and proper receipts and accountings were maintained. The patrolman problem in question started a rowl and his friends joined in. With misstatements and accusations flying, the truth got lost in a blizzard of political theatrics. My administrative error came when I stated we sold six instead of seven. No big deal, but then you weren't in Galena Park. You would have thought I had stolen and sold National Security Secrets or had urinated on the Alamo. The mayor, I believe, saw that his time was short, so he was going to attempt to save himself. We talked about the issue and he ask me "what would you do?". I told him that not allowing me to comment and his refusing to comment was not the way to go, that he should just stand up and tell the truth. This was a no big deal situation and the voters would see that. It was at this point that it hit me just where he was coming from. The mayor looked straight at me and said " yes I know you would tell the truth, and it is a no big deal, but then you aren't running for re-election". Well, kiss my grits, there it was. Don't support your Chief. Don't support the efforts of the Chief. Don't tell the truth. Don't worry about the future or present position of the Chief. Don't worry about what is right, or what is wrong. Don't worry about who the real problems are.

So, like I said, I chunked it to them, that very day. Now some would say I should have stayed. For what? Until I got another position? Maybe it would blow over. Maybe the old mayor would not win. Maybe the bad officers would have joint seizures and pass on. Right. Maybe pigs will fly some day also. So I took my little booboo and departed, having become smarter for the ordeal.

So, the old mayor won. He paid the old and re-stored Chief a bonus. He also paid the patrolman, now Assistant Chief, a big bonus. For sterling and life saving police work? Not hardly. The gambling trips continued until finally someone with enough juice figured it out and complained. Other less than savory and legal practices re-emerged and life went on.

Oh, I cannot pass without mentioning this. The Chief, Mr. J, was a near illiterate. The Patrolman, Mr. P, was as devious and consumed with himself as any I have seen. Mr. P wasn't satisfied with being Assistant Chief, he wanted to be Chief. Within a year of the old being restored, Mr. P began an effort to can the Chief, Mr. J. With the blessing of the Mayor, he succeeded, and forced Mr. J to take a hike. No honor among thieves so to speak. The only trouble with being that type of "animal" is that you have to constantly watch your back side, because those who live by that creed, will also be the victim of that creed. I cannot say I will be saddened.

I went to the house and filled my wife in on the latest antics and that I had re-signed. Without any immediate prospects, I went to hunting a position. After all, there is no creditor walking that gives two hoots in hell about anyone that owes them money doing the right thing and not being able to pay. For a period of time I worked as an insurance fraud investigator, watching various smucks claim injuries and disability monies, only to be caught on tape mowing the lawn, swimming, and various other activities. For the most part this type of investigative work entails many long hours of sitting and waiting, being bored to tears, unable to go the restroom for fear of missing the target in action, and being turned in to the local police as suspicious. Yet, most of the time, the yoyo target exposes themselves, not literally, and you get the evidence needed to shut down their spurious claims and to even prosecute some of them. It does have its lighter moments.

Now, there are those in the State of Texas that when ask about me will say that I am hard headed. That is true, but not to the degree that I am obtuse. This most recent and bad tasting experience was not of such a nature as to sour me on my chosen profession, although there were some close friends who questioned my sanity for wanting to stay in. I still had a lot of years left in me and I continued to know that my abilities were needed, somewhere. So, the hunt continued. Mike Mason is one of my true friends and I cannot say enough nice about this retired U.S. Navy man and head of security for a chemical company in Harris County. He is stand up dude. Anyway, Mike had been seeking a similar position before landing in the feedbag of private industry, and had applied to various cities to be their Chief. Mike called me one evening and said that the City of Donna was looking for a tough Chief to clean up their mess and they had called Mike and Mike turned it down, due to his recent ascendancy to the upper financial bracket as a Security Manager. However, Mike said he told the City Manager of me and that I could handle the difficulty. So, the City Manager, Robert Diaz De Leon, and I talked on the telephone. Within a couple days I drove down to Donna for further discussions. Now, Donna sits right down on the U.S. and Mexico border, between McAllen and Harlingen. It is Indian territory, if you know what I mean. I had known about Donna and the area for many years, stretching back to my Fed days, as keeping track of corruption was a necessity. So I was somewhat knowledgeable about the problems and had worked in the Valley before and understood the mindset of most of the residents.

It was early August of 1996 and the drive from Corpus Christi to McAllen and then Donna is basically a desolate and boring affair. It was also hotter than a grasshopper on a skillet. It was almost like driving off in to a third, or even, fourth world country. Poverty, for many, and slovenliness for many more, was the order of the day. Crime was rampant. Narcotics flowed like water, and corruption was a way of life. There has been times when I thought it would have been better for most everyone if someone would chop the Valley off of the bottom end of Texas and give it to Mexico, but then the mentalities would only cross the newly established boundary and re-infest the new Valley. So, there has to be a concerted and continuing effort to exorcise that value system, because if it spreads and becomes entrenched across the country, our society is in deep trouble. In the months and days that laid ahead I was to witness and to oppose some of the damnedest situations and individuals that I had ever met and it was to be an education that if you bottle it you sell and make a fortune. On the other hand, it was to be a time and series of events that most common sense and logically thinking people would not understand. Hell, I am not sure I understand it, and I lived through it, if only barely.

We sacrifice our ethics for harmony.

James T. Reese

CHAPTER EIGHT

THE FIRE

Armed with fore knowledge of the area and the city and its attendant problems, I arrived at the appointed hour at the City Hall for the City of Donna. I should have realized that the word was out about who was being interviewed by the City Manager, but if I did, I don't think it registered very hard, and the surveillance slipped under my radar screen. At 8:00 AM I was shown in to the City Manager's office by a not hard to look at secretary who was more than amply endowed by her maker. After being momentarily distracted, we got down to the business at hand. Robert was a salt and pepper haired man about my age who held a degree in Engineering and built bridges, before entangling himself in the idiocy of municipal politics, but my impression of him, was that Robert was an honest man, even if somewhat out of his league in his newly chosen position. The surprising part of this meeting was that there was very little exchange of information, questions, positions or expectations. What it turned out to be was a fifty-five minute diatribe by Robert about the ills, sins and corruptive nature of his police department. Robert made no bones about it, he had one hell of a problem with the police department and he had to have someone who was not afraid to step in and clean it out. You notice that I said clean it out, and not clean it up. Robert made it abundantly clear that the city knew that the level of corruption was bad, that there was theft, narcotics, civil rights violations and many other problems perpetrated by the officers. Robert went on to say that not a single agency in the entire area would talk to the Donna PD because "no one" trusted the Donna PD and its officers. Robert's passion for the topic was undeniable. He got down right ugly and used expletives to describe the situation and his opinion of the personnel. This was a shocker to say the least. I had never run into a city manager that so excoriated his police as Robert did. Now that is not to say they did not deserve it, but it was apparent from the examples given by Robert that the situation in Donna was even worse than I had previously known about. Jesus! Did I really want in this mess? Just before nine the telephone rang and Robert cut our meeting short due to some kind of emergency that had jumped up. So, with the parting goodbyes and the promise to call me, I left, and I again missed the surveillance, or rather it did not register as it should have. All the way home, which took considerable time, I ran all of this information through my mind and played a few dozen what if games. I was looking for potential solutions and at the same time was trying to identify potential pitfalls. Obviously, the number of alternatives and scenarios were seemingly unlimited. What else was also obvious was that taking the position would be dangerous, both physically and professionally. However, that trait to which I previously admitted, reared its head. Yep, I am hard headed. More importantly, to this set of facts, is that I love a challenge and as crass as it may sound, I loved to be needed and to help those who were incapable of helping themselves. By the time I got home I had pretty much made up my mind. Now all I had to do was convince my wife. It would have to be by agreement, because she too would be subject to a set of conditions and problems that she had not faced before. Now, I have to say, my wife is a real trooper. She has followed me from camp to camp over the years, moving fourteen times and on a couple of occasions, living in conditions that were almost intolerable. We had seen a lot of adversity, privately and professionally, and she had never really been afraid before, because she knew I would take care of her and the kids. Yet, I foresaw that this situation would not be like what we had seen in the past. The dynamics were going to be more rigorous in many ways. So she had a say and that was that. Getting back to Houston took about eight hours. Our discussion lasted well after midnight, and then resumed the next evening for several more hours. It was not an easy decision. We had hoped to remain in one place, to buy a home, and grow old gracefully. My wife, Betty, had a great job with a medical doctor that she really liked, and even though it hurt to move, and for me to be the cause of her having to move again, she agreed. Within a couple days Robert was on the phone wanting to know how quick I could get down there because he really needed me. That was Thursday evening and on Sunday I pulled out of the driveway and headed south. Off to slay the dragons and make the world safe for children and old women. Ha! Double Ha! Little did I know the extent of treachery, deceit and falsehood that people would go to in order to protect their pathetic circumstances.

The first few days I would live in a motel, not for the first time, and look for an apartment. Preferably one where I did not have to shoot my way in and out of everyday. On Monday morning, August 27, 1996, at 8:00 AM I was sitting at City Hall waiting for Robert to show up at work and mulling over the prospects which faced me. I had spent the weekend driving around the city, looking over the lay of the land so to speak, getting my bearings and observing various activities. I was able to monitor various police communications channels and paid attention to the number and types of calls that were being dispatched by the Donna PD. With the help of a city map I bought at a local convenience store, better known as a stop and rob, I began to learn the streets and occasionally eased by a patrol unit on a call. The city was nothing to shout about, cosmetically speaking, and the level of traffic was pretty heavy.

I don't know of any police executive that would disagree with the premise that you generally tell the level of crime in a city and the level of respect for the law and institutions in a city by the way people adhere to the traffic code. It is an indicator, although I know there are academic types who would dispute such a presumptive position. All I can say is, academics and real life don't often coincide. Anyway, it became very obvious that the residents of dear ole Donna did not give a hoot in hades for the traffic laws of the State. Light controlled intersection devices were pistol targets and to be ignored whenever suitable to the individual whimsy. Stop signs literally meant Squeal Tires on Pavement or Sure, Tease Our Police. What was more interesting was the number of vehicles I saw operated with out of date registrations and inspection stickers. Beer bottles and cans lined the gutter along the curb of the downtown city park and bandstand area. At night this "park" was a park and drink spot. The hotrod exhibitions went on up and down the main drag as if NASCAR was sanctioning them. Where in the world were the patrol units? This was definitely going to be interesting.

Mr. Robert Diaz DeLeon came in huffing and puffing. Seems they had some kind of water problem that had service all messed up to a good portion of the city. Now, don't forget the water problem being mentioned as it will play a crucial role in the events to come. No, I am not kidding. Anyway, Robert and I go in to his office. I received a few of the obligatory forms for Federal income tax withholding and retirement to fill out, but the majority of the conversation reverted quickly to a continuation of the subject matter from the first interview. Robert made no bones about it, the department was corrupt, even rogue, and he wanted it cleaned out. In fact, I was told to "do whatever you have to, to clean it up, and I will support you". After an hour or so, we were joined by the City Attorney, David Martinez. He was young, affable and, like Robert, concerned about the future of the department. Robert and I discussed potential resolutions to the problems and it was agreed, upon my suggestion, that for the near future, there would be only one person within the city government that I would inform of all the situations and actions undertaken to meet the mandate, and that was Robert himself. Martinez agreed, not so much because he wanted to, but I don't think he knew any other idea to suggest. The need for this revolved around security of information and investigations. I did not know whom within the department or outside the department that I could trust. What Robert did not know, is that I did not intend, at least for the short term, to even tell him everything. I wasn't sure that I could even trust Robert. The conversation about narcotics, civil rights violations, rape of female prisoners and a laundry list of other violations continued. If Robert was putting on act about what he said and what he wanted done, it was a performance without equal in history. We also discussed the issue of internal personnel and who was in what positions and the fact that one had applied for Chief, and how that person would receive the news of being passed over. The Captain, and Acting Chief, was Clemente. According to what Robert said Clemente would never have a chance to be Chief in Donna as long as Robert was there. He was described as a weasel, do nothing, spineless and only being in the department and advanced to Captain because of his parents. It was damn sure not on account of his capabilities. On that score I advised that I would work with him and see what we could do to improve his performance and capabilities. That was to be an unreachable fairy tale.

It was about ten o'clock in the morning when Clemente came to the office, ostensibly to see if Robert had any marching orders for him that day, but in reality, curiousity was probably killing him, as was the need to collect any information he could about the new boss. Robert brought him and introduced him. Robert wanted Clemente to show me around, get all the records available that I may request and in general do whatever was needed to get me up to speed and in tune to the department, personnel, administration and operations. Clemente, well, he was whipped, and that was obvious. I doubt if he had any more backbone than a jelly fish. His ability to orally communicate was, well let's say, it was limited. With a handshake synonymous with cold linguini, I was not impressed. Yet, he was to meet me at the PD at 1:00 PM to commence the transition. In the meantime I was to accompany Robert and David to a small local restaurant where we were to have lunch with the Mayor and as many city council members as could attend. It was described as a get to know everyone get together. At the same time, Robert advised that a public reception had been planned at the Palms where I would be introduced to the community. So far, Robert was up front, cooperative and doing all those things you would anticipate a good city manager to do for a new Chief. I was on the payroll and brother I would earn every nickel of the salary. Oh, that reminds me. We discussed the salary and benefits in the presence of the City Attorney. The City of Donna, according to both of them, was in dire financial straits. In fact, they were on the verge of bankruptcy. That was a gem of information that no one had mentioned before and came as a disquieting shock on that morning. We agreed that I should make $45,000, but Robert was not sure they had it and that he could sell that price tag to the council. So, being a cooperative sort and not a mercenary, I offered to start at $40,000 per annum and that at the end of six months, presuming that I was doing a good job, still alive and had not departed for brighter climes, Robert would raise it to $45,000. Robert beamed at that idea and told me that I would earn a lot of points for that gesture. So, it was done. We loaded up in Roberts vehicle and drove to the restaurant. Inside sat two uniformed police officers. They had known where to be to get a look at the new boss and both of them would be entwined in investigations and actions that I would have to run in the immediate future. I knew then that there was at least one leak or source of information for the officers inside the staff at City Hall. That was not good and yet also not unexpected. What I wanted to know is where the guy with the bucket of grease was at. The one that would be greasing the path I had to travel. They would hand out condoms at the schools for safe sexual encounters, a safety net so to speak, to protect their children. Not thinking about the safer alternative of course. Yet, for the Chief of Police in this denizen of dirty deeds, there would be no safety net. None, nada, zip, zilch.

At the luncheon I met the Mayor, Mrs. Hilda Adame, a very likable lady who had been in local government for years in both Weslaco and now in Donna. Estella Villegas was another member of the council and I quickly realized she did not mind speaking her mind and she did not take crud off of anyone. Of course she was well enough off and secure enough she did not have to worry about it, but she also really cared about the future and betterment of the city. She was a trip and would become a good friend to me. Then there was Adan Hernandez, a local businessman, who let me know in a hurry that he did not like the Captain, Clemente, and that he knew of some of the narcotics actions that officers were involved in. He would become a source of information. Then came the two sneaks, liberals, anti-establishment types. One was a school teacher, or at least that is what he got paid to be, and the other had something to do with insurance. They would be problems down the road. Not to your face, but under the table and behind your back. The lunch was cordial and went well and as we were leaving I just tossed all caution to the wind and ask the Mayor a point blank question. The question was, is there anyone in the department or the city that is off limits from discipline or the law? At first, she was not sure what I was asking, then it hit her, and she replied, "No, you do what ever you have to". Now I knew that such magnanimous words don't always last, but I had her on record, at least for the near future. Mrs. Villegas, well she was more to the point. She wanted Clemente and others in jail. All Adan said specifically was that I should be careful and if he could help to let him know. As for the other two, it was platitudes and bullshit. The council, if you couldn't tell, was split three to two, in favor of the moderate/conservative side and both the City Manager and City Attorney supported the majority. Of course, not being engraved in stone, that would not last.

As a law enforcement executive, or even just a law enforcement officer, unless you had been living in a cave for the past several years, you would know of the massive problems within the New Orleans Police Department. Vastly underpaid, working on the good old boy system and with little or no quality direction, the department had sunk to a dismal low. Officers were regularly involved in murder, extortion, narcotics trafficking, bribery and more. It had gotten so blatant and bad that the FBI had a task force that was working nothing but criminal acts by police, public corruption. The new Mayor vowed to fix it and brought in a new Chief of Police with quality credentials to clean it up. Richard Pennington knew coming in what he faced. It was to be a bedeviling task, but one that could be resolved. His department was much bigger than the one I had in Donna, but many of the problems were the same. The major difference was, in terms of percentages, the Donna PD had more officers involved in criminality than New Orleans. I had wondered what kind of task Richard was faced with when I heard he was going to take over in New Orleans, but now I had a good idea. In one memorandum that I sent to the Assistant U.S. Attorney who was overseeing the Donna investigation, I remarked about that very symbiosis.

When I got to the PD that afternoon Clemente showed me around and then let me know that my office was the empty one out front, and publicly accessible. Well, that wasn't going to work, but I chose to bide my time on that issue. Then, the city vehicle that was to be mine, was a Tahoe, but Clemente did not want to give it up for a week. Again, and maybe mistakenly, I chose to go along, not wanting to create waves on the very first day. In retrospect, he took those two acts as a sign of weakness and it would lead to other tests, but the outcomes would not be the same.

The department organization was a joke. The administrative controls were almost non-existent. There was no departmental manual or guidelines for operations other than a loose collection of memos, most of which were short lived and often in conflict with each other. Now, if you have never written, from scratch, a departmental manual, with general orders and special orders and the like, it will be very difficult to imagine the task, but I am here to tell you it will consume a great deal of time and research to make it right and functional. So that was a task that was at the top of my list.

That very morning, before I had met anyone in the department or had been to the station, the officers had commenced an effort to get rid of me. It is called a letter of no confidence, which they think and many others around the State think, is a great method by which they can control who is Chief. For some crazy reason, cities have given credence to this upside down method of human resources recruitment and retention, thus bolstering the mis-guided attitude of the personnel. The radical type in the department started the move, the Lieutenant held the meeting in his office, and it was all spurred on by Clemente. Needless to say, Clemente was not a happy camper in that he did not get the top job. After only two days of observing and reviewing the operation, it was not hard to understand that Clemente did not know a damn thing about what he was suppose to be doing. The Lieutenant only showed up and gave little or no direction. Three of the four Sergeants were incompetent, lazy and crooked as a bag of snakes, and all but three of the patrolman were as worthless as a side saddle on a hog. All in all fourteen out of twenty personnel should be in jail, not putting others in jail. It had taken years and years for the department to achieve this pinnacle of disarray and I knew it would not be fixed overnight or even in just a few months.

First came a meeting called by me of all personnel. The message was clear. We are police officers. We are suppose to enforce the law, not violate it. I let them know in no uncertain terms that it was bad, that I would not play the mindless games, and that if anyone screwed up, he would rue the day. That meeting was a week in to my administration and I had been physically and mentally challenged, on no less than six occasions, by officers. In just the first week. It was time, in my humble opinion to take the reins and start turning this wild beast around. Did they believe me? Naw! Not at first, but then the son of an retired and influential Deputy Sheriff decided to sexually abuse a female inmate. He ordered her to take her clothes off so he could check for weapons. Now, it did not matter that she was already in the cell from the night before. He thought, or so he claimed, that she was armed. By the time I finished the investigation and the paper work, he only had three days left on his probationary period. I took the recommendation to the City Manager to bounce him for failure to meet the probationary requirements. It was signed. I called him in and handed to him. You would have thought I was the villain and he berated me with four letter words on his way out the door. The Captain was sitting there and you could see it written all over him, he did not like it. Tough bananas. One down, thirteen to go. But that was not the end of it. The first test of my authority and actions came when the retired Deputy, who thought he had lots of drag, called Adan and suggested that his son should be returned to the department. Adan said, to his credit, that it was the Chief's call and the call of the City Manager. The pressure dropped off. And, before I forget, you should know that the fired officer had been a Deputy, but had more than a few sexually oriented complaints against him, that the Sheriff's office conveniently lost and or would not share with any one else.

I am a prolific note taker. During the days I would come across all types of information that would boggle the mind and I had started a formal investigation, the only copy of which was on my computer at the apartment. I soon changed that though as my apartment was a target, so the report was on a 3.5 disk that I carried in my breast wallet. It, the report, was growing by leaps and bounds. The next issue that gave me a leg up came when one night three officers got in a fight with a suspect and his wife and one officer got hurt in the melee. The dispatcher was under directions to notify me of any serious situation so I could monitor it, so I got dressed and went to the scene. Upon approaching I noticed two guys in a truck, watching the scene, but I did not think more of it, at the time. To make a long story short, the two men were the Captain and his buddy, the city Humane Officer, who was also under my direction. It turns out the Captain was drinking at home with the dog catcher and they drove a city unit to the store and bought more beer and on the way back stopped to watch the fight and drink. Bad move, for Clemente anyway. I did the investigation and confronted Clemente. I had already stacked a bunch of work on him that I knew he could not handle, but that, in his position, he should be able to handle, so he was already displeased with me. On this day, I chewed his butt pretty hard for driving and drinking, driving a city unit and drinking, and drinking while he sat and watched officers of his agency engaged in a confrontation and he did nothing. I did not cut him any slack. He was mad, scared and intimidated, all at the same time, but with a constitution of jello, he had no choice that was viable. Within a week, or so, he decided to leave the department in lieu of starting his own business. While I "appeared" to try and dissuade him, it was a feeble effort to say the least and I was actually thrilled. Clemente, I had learned by now, was the ring leader of the corruption within the Donna Police Department and was connected to illicit operations around the county. Clemente knew his days under me were limited, to say the least, and I don't doubt that he thought he could beat me if he was working from the outside. So Clemente opened his little business, which was to be short lived, and he also filed to run for the city council. There was to be a steady flow of on duty and off duty officers going and coming from his so called business. Think they were plotting? At the same time, my internal investigation was picking up steam and information. I had gone to several of the area agencies seeking any information and assistance they might provide. Most were reluctant to talk, much less give up anything of value, because they did not know if I was part of the problem or not. Yet, with the passage of time and persistence, I began to convince them by my actions that a new deal was in town and the old was not to be condoned or tolerated anymore. Two down, twelve to go.

The evidence room in Donna was also a flying joke. There was a big walk in safe with a heavy steel door and combination lock. Of course, everybody and his brother had the combination. There was no log in procedures, accountability procedures or anything. You just did your own thing. So I changed the combination, established an almost airtight system and put the CID Corporal in charge. I let him know that if anything went wrong it was his cheeks that would feel the fire. His conformity was acquired not out of professionalism, duty, the law or anything lofty, but rather the mere fact that the blow torch was turned his way and my finger was on the trigger. I freely admit, leadership through fear is not the best way or even a good way, but when you are faced with extraordinary circumstances, you do what has to be done to achieve the end required. Then a turning point arrived or was summed by my actions. Which ever, it was welcomed, to say the least.

I am sitting in my office when two men arrived and wanted to meet with me. It turns out they are DPS Narcotics from Harlingen. They started asking questions and wanting to provide assistance in the inventory of the department's evidence room Now I may not be the smartest person in the world, but it took me all of one minute to realize there was more to this encounter than met the eye. So I started asking hard ball questions and getting answers like, we cannot discuss that, or someone else will call you soon, and etc. So by the time we finished, I told these two agents, you have told me more by what you haven't said that by what you have said. In truth they were looking for a way to get in the evidence vault to look for evidence for their case without tipping their hand. In addition, they were checking me out for their boss, Lt. Beto Diaz. Having achieved an unspoken understanding, I agreed they should help do the inventory, and they would have their Lt get in touch with me. In a day or so the inventory commenced and I did not worry, because the DPS troops would make sure it was right and anything amiss would be brought to me right away, and the Corporal, well, he was another sneak, so he would not challenge it. Besides, he still remembered the blow torch. Then I got a call from Beto, wanting to meet. From that point on, the Federal, DPS and internal cases melded together and things began to move. The temperature was rising, and all the crooks were feeling the heat, albeit indirectly. No one in the city, but myself, knew about the external investigation and I could not tell them. In fact, if I had been able to tell all of what I had learned, it may have made a major difference in the events that would bring several tenures to an end, including my own.

Now, I told you not to forget the water. A police department and its officers are universally expected to solve all types of problems, but in Donna I encountered a situation that was totally foreign to law enforcement, but I became a target. For more years than anyone really knows, or will admit to, a good portion of the residents of the city had been receiving water and sewer services, without ever having to pay for them. Why? Well, it seems that previous administrations had been rather lax in performing their responsibilities and far too many citizens had water lines, but no water meters. Or, the meters had been broken since who knows when. The city had contracted with a private corporation out of Houston to come in and install new lines, put in new meters and basically manage the water system and the collection of the revenues. Of course, for those who had not paid for water in no telling when, the receipt of water bills was unsettling, to say the least. Now logic states you have to pay for running water, but logic in the valley is an oxymoron for many. So the idiots got together with Lulac and formed a citizens group to protest the water rates, the city manager, Eco Systems and whatever else was available because those targets were picking on the poor downtrodden residents. Pay for a city water service, that is ridiculous. And the battle was engaged. No amount of common sense talking would do any good. So there were protest and confrontations, destruction of water meters, lines and a raft of more illegal hookups.

On the day of my first meeting with the Assistant United States Attorney regarding the corruption investigation, I was informed that the radicals were going to stage a march through town, on the busiest highway, to Eco Systems for a protest and then on to city hall for another protest. Just ducky! I informed the appropriate personnel to provide a two unit escort for the protestors, towards keeping any of the marchers from getting run over. Knowing the mentality at work, I also instructed an officer to discreetly video tape the protests, just in case things got out of hand and we needed some visual confirmation as to who did what. The meeting with the Assistant U.S. Attorney went well, after I had to shake a tail.

Persons were curious as to where I was going. By the time I got back to the city, the crowd of about 200 had moved over to city hall and were demanding to see the city manager. He was somewhere else on city business. There was no interference with the protestors and except for a few of the ring leaders, it was as peaceful as could have been expected. They blocked the sidewalks and doors, restricting others from attending to their jobs or their personal business and that is when I ask the leader, L. Rodriguez, if they could move off the sidewalk to allow others to enter and leave city hall. The response was four letter words and abusive accusations. Fortunately, a woman from Lulac agreed and they moved off the sidewalk. The city manager arrived and he was quickly surrounded by a yelling crowd. It got a little rough and very verbally ugly, but no action was taken at that time. The crowd vowed to come to city hall that night for the council meeting to confront the mayor and council. Now the council chambers only holds, by ordinance, forty individuals. At 7:00 PM the room was filled. The council was in place and here came Rodriguez, demanding that all of "his" followers be allowed in the room. The fact that there was no way for another one hundred and fifty people to fit in that room made no difference. The noise level increased and finally Mayor Adame told Rodriguez that he and his followers could line up in the hall, but only on one side, so that people could still come and go. I am sure that this rabble rousing "victim" was going to do just that. The city manager sent me out to make sure and that is where it got really ugly. Three times I attempted to talk to Mr. Rodriguez and each time, he butted me with his shoulder and head. Each time I took a step or two back and again attempted to talk to him. He advised me in the most colorful terms that they did not have to listen to an sob ^***&^%%$(* from east Texas and he exhalted his followers to follow him. We all were on the verge of not a protest, but an ugly confrontation. I had been assaulted three times. The city council meeting was being interrupted and interfered with and there was a rising risk factor. Other officers were present as were many other citizens. The fourth time I tried to talk to Mr. Rodriguez about where he and his people were to stand, he butted me again. This time, enough was enough. I arrested him and had him removed from the city hall. They had come to create an incident and now there had been one. Was I wrong? Not by the law and common sense. Yet, others would claim so.

The rabble rousers called the media and here came the television stations with their remote trucks. Rodriguez was quickly let out of jail by the city magistrate and the press statements were flying fast and loose. The city manager thanked me for putting a stop to what he called was a mob on the verge of rioting. Yet, the war was just getting started. All because these idiots who want everything for nothing, did not like having to pay for the water supplied by the city and used by themselves. Oh, by the way, there was a lot of people in the crowed who were not citizens of Donna. They had been brought in. Practiced participants at raising hell.

The external and internal investigation of the Donna PD and its upstanding personnel continued and widened. Two more cases of officers sexually abusing and even raping female inmates were uncovered. Two brothers, and former officers, then working at the Donna ISD, had been overseeing a juvenile gang that was ripping off everything they could from school buildings, with the help of the keys from the brothers. Oh, the brothers were in charge of security. There was the police sergeant who called a narcotics dealers house and warned him that he was under investigation and surveillance by narcotics agents. It just so happened that the undercover agent was in the dope dealers house at the time the call came in. That had to be tense time for the officer, but fortunately, he was not found out. That long time Sergeant was definitely going to have to go, either in to unemployment or preferably, jail. I found that citizens were coming to the PD and advising that they would be out of town for x amount of time and requested a watch be put on their homes during their absence. This information was taken by two of the officers and given to juveniles who would burglarize the empty homes and steal everything that wasn't nailed down or painted. The officers would split the take with the kids. No, I am not kidding. Then, we have two officers who would stop narcotics traffickers, force them to reveal what they were transporting or where they had it concealed, rip the dealer off for his dope, and his money, and send him on his way. Who was going to tell on them? The officers took the ripped off dope to a brother, who sold it for them and they split the money. Clemente, that astute servant of the people, would be advised when a load of narcotics was coming through town and he would call all of the on duty personnel in to the station about half an hour before the load moved through the city and keep them there for about a half an hour after the load was gone. On other occasions, police patrol units would run the front door for the load vehicles to get them through town without any hassles. Any information that was obtained about narcotics investigations was quickly passed on to the various narcotics violators that lived in and around the city. For these acts, and many others, the officers were paid by the narcotics violators. Clemente was in a ring with a Hidalgo County Sheriff Deputy and a DPS Trooper. That end of the business ran loads of drugs through the Border Patrol checkpoint, in police vehicles. The take was good. At city hall, there were at least two sources that provided all of the juicy information they could come up with. The city magistrate (judge), the use of such title was nauseating, was an individual who later became a suspect in the murder of his mother-in-law. In the meantime, he exercised his judicial prowess by offering to dismiss citations for women who provided him with sexual favors. YUK! Most citations issued to residents of Donna were dismissed. No reason, no justification, just dismissed. Oh, it was undoubtedly of personal interest to the "judge" since these violators would be eligible to vote in the next election. There was the fire department employee and a PD dispatcher, both of whom were married to someone else, that were getting it on in the dispatch office. The selling of official police documents, and on and on and on…

Now you are probably thinking, naw this can't be, well I am here to tell you, and there are others who can support it, it was going on. Try this one on. A fat slob of a Sergeant is riding with me to go pick up another vehicle. The sergeant begins talking of his past experiences and brags, in front of the Chief of all people, that the Sergeant had been a bodyguard for a major narcotics smuggler living in Matamoros, Mexico. I liked to have fell out of the vehicle at this unsolicited revelation and the Sergeant thought nothing of it. I still ask myself, why in the hell did I agree to try and clean up this mess? How in the blazes did this guy ever get hired? One violation here, one violation there and the resolution would not have been too hard, but there were more violations, daily, than you could shake a stick at and I was all alone with no one to count on when the stuff really got tight.

I don't recall how many bars or open heart surgery establishments were in town, but they all had a little dope dealing going on and prostitutes working the customers. Upon my mentioning that we were going to pay all of them a visit one night, a Sergeant remarked, in earnest, "We can't do that". When I inquired as to why not, he seriously stated, "Because the bar owners don't like it". So there was another message, stay out of the bars or we (the bar owners) will make you. Well, not being real conversant with dictated terms, I was more determined than ever to go pay them all a call. So we loaded up and went to each one. Of course, they knew we were coming so there were no violations about, but even for the leak from inside the PD, the visits delivered a message. The next time, it was a sneak attack. No prior warnings from the PD snitch and those visits were not appreciated. One portly type proprietor was more directly vocal than most and we exchanged words. In sum, I told him I would make a sub-station out of his place if he desired and we would see how things went from there. That was enough said, even for a dummy. The trouble in the bars dropped like a rock from then on.

I have always been a firm believer in enforcing the traffic laws, as they are a window in to the more serious violations within a community and they often help solve more serious offenses. That would be especially possible in a city that sat on the crossroads of major trafficking alleys. So, with a little private pre-event planning and the best wishes of the city manager, I started throwing up impromptu roadblocks on certain avenues, to check for current vehicle registrations, drivers licenses, inspection stickers and insurance. This had been prompted by a rising tide of complaints from citizens involved in accidents with Donna citizens, and others, and who did not have any of the above. It was funny to watch. Cars backed up for blocks, surprised at what was going on, wondering what was going on and trying to find a way to turn off or around and to get out of there. The amazing part was that official estimates stated that about forty to fifty percent of those driving, did not have a license, registration, inspection or insurance. Even more amazing is that when I checked all of the officers, there were eleven of them that did not have a current drivers license, insurance, inspection sticker or registration, or all of the above. They were all given thirty days to achieve a lawful status or else, and would you believe they got mad about it. On top of that, there was a booming market in the valley for forged and or stolen registrations, inspection stickers and proof of insurance documents. It would cost you $50 for a phony on average and would only last until an officer got a hold of it and tore it up and put it in evidence. Not real bright by any stretch of the imagination, but far too many felt it was easier to do it that way and violate the law than do it legal. The mindset of many that lived there was just mind boggling. There is an old saying that fits this description and it goes "there are people who will climb a tree to tell a lie, when they could stand on the ground and tell the truth". What it boiled down to is, if they could find a way to get anything for free, get around the law, ignore the law or whatever else took their fancy, they would and everyone else be damned. Such as the individuals whose only job was to go out and look for someone to sue. A driver, a store, the city, whoever. It was a 365 day a year circus. In fact, the valley area of Texas ranks second in the United States in law suits filed. The southern portion of Florida ranks number one.

Of course, all of this banal courtroom activity could not go on if it were not for the acquiescence of the judges and the juries, which are ultimately picked to hear such droll accusations. They permit and encourage the conduct by individuals looking for money and the only true winners in any such tomfoolery are the lawyers. A lady, whose family has lived in the valley for three generations, and whose business has been painstakingly built over those generations, commented, "if you live in the valley, you are going to be sued, it is just a cost of living and doing business here". That is a sad indictment of the mindset of the litigative community.

Okay, we are about four months in to the new regime at Donna PD, and the opposition is continuously seeking a way to unseat the new Chief. On the other hand, there is a growing number of citizens in the city and from around the city who are telephoning in or writing in to express their appreciation for the new ideology and the positive work. I had made friends with two FBI Special Agents who worked on narcotics and public corruption and we hit it off real good. There was an ATF Agent, a Secret Service Agent and quite a few U.S. Border Patrol officers and managers that were all buying in to the "new" Donna PD and we met and talked when ever possible. Now, I am definitely not the savior of the world, but I do know my business pretty good, and I have to admit that it did make me feel good and that all the heat was worth it, when these other professionals gave me their verbal and moral support. We were doing something right. The development of intelligence was also increasing, particularly on narcotics, and I was regularly sharing that information with the DEA, the Task Force, DPS Narcotics and the FBI. Smugglers and dealers were getting popped, drugs seized and large sums of money were being placed in evidence control. The police officers in Donna were beginning to see the light, not of their wrong road activities, but the fact that this Chief was not going to back off and wasn't going to run.

Two "men" tried to wire my city vehicle one night around 2 A.M. and a neighbor spotted them. The city managers car was turned in to swiss cheese and the number of telephoned threats to my wife served to keep me on my toes and to not to become too infatuated with the good words that were being said. In fact, if there was any doubt, a fat Sergeant walked up to me one morning and uneceremoniously stated that "he did not think I would be very hard to whip". Now coming out of the blue, such a comment will get your attention. Blocking the hall with his girth, and waiting to see what my response would be, I took two steps back, squared myself and, trying to keep it light, said, "well, the next time you see your feet, let me know and we can test your theory." He was surprised at the response and I have to admit, so was I. Anyway, the mercury fell in his thermometer, and he went on out the back door.

It took a pretty good while to complete the inventory of the evidence vault and the results were not surprising at all. First, there were various quantities of marijuana and cocaine missing. Missing? Not hardly, it had been purloined for the financial betterment of the poor underpaid cops. Weapons, always good for bartering or quick cash, were also in on the "disappearance" list. We also came across a bunch of court issued destruction orders for various weapons and other items that were discovered in an old and mostly unused safe over in the CID offices. They had all been signed and sworn to that the item listed on each had been destroyed. Only trouble was, they had not been destroyed. The current CID Sergeant had falsified the documents. On top of that pressure cooker came the knowledge that he was using cocaine and alcohol at a fast clip. Two more down and ten to go. The Lieutenant, being totally useless and unable to withstand any of his assigned work load was having a hard time. Then he takes a city unit home and proceeds to wreck it. In fact he wreck not only the city unit, but tore up another drivers vehicle in the process. He decided that it was time to give up the ghost and resigned, just ahead of the axe. Five down. Within the first nine months, seven offenders had gotten or were shown, by various methods, the gate. No loss and the outlook was picking up. The Federal Grand Jury was meeting with more regularity now and I periodically had to go to McAllen for meetings with Terry Leonard and the agents in charge of that investigation. At one point, I actually began to believe that we could win this situation and in the end the city and PD would be better than when we started. Yet, the opposition had not gone to sleep.

On the scene pops up two individuals, one male and one female, who decided to run for the city council slots being vacated by or up for election of Adan and Estella. The city manager, Mayor and I sure hated to see that turn of events. If these two well known extremist who sided with the previous mentality of how things should be done in Donna, got in, the control would shift and the good guys, so to speak, would be out in the cold. The city manager and I discussed this and he was cozying up to the them in an effort to lay a foundation to extend the control and make sure things did not go back to hell in a wash tub. Me, I was not assured. In fact, the Mayor talked to me one day and wanted to know how quick I could finish cleaning the situation out so as to blunt some of the local support. I told her, as before, that it took a damn long time for it to get this way, and if we going to adhere to the rule of law and procedures, we still had a ways to go. At least a few months. Sure, I knew what she wanted, but to provide it without procedural basis and fact would only invite more recriminations and more trouble, and even a crook in blue has the right to fair treatment. Yeah, makes no sense, but that is the system and even though parts of the system irritate me to no end, it is the best there is and I will uphold it until someone comes up with a better one.

The old man who assaulted me at the council meeting, through his even more radical lawyer son, sued me and the city for, get this, $9.5 million. That was a calculated event and added fuel to the fire in the local scene. A CID officer got nailed for attempting to extort an assault rifle from a dummie in jail, offering to have the case dismissed if the dummie gave the officer the rifle. ATF did not think it was too funny and the officer got the pink slip shortly thereafter. That cut the dope dealer ripoff crew down to ostensibly one now. Those who were no longer with the PD, a few inside the PD and a list of yoyo's in the community who liked the old ways, began a new effort. A public relations campaign, using signs on trailers, falsified accusations nailed to telephone poles and much more. There was even a bomb threat called in to an elementary school, that required evacuation and search, and then a flyer was found the next morning on many doors and poles, stating that the Chief had called in the threat. Stupid as all this was, and believe it or not, it began to work. Even more ridiculous, was fact that I had ask all of the personnel, at the beginning, to put down their views of the department, how to make it better, what they would like to see and so on, on paper. In the first nine months of the some fifty odd suggestions and desires, I had moved, with the city manager to correct or install various of those goals, numbering about thirty. The effort was not intended to placate or curry favor, but to build respect, comradeship and to let them all know that the Chief did care about the personnel. One of those suggestions, came from all of the dispatchers and a few of the other officers, that the front door security, at night, was terrible and that anyone could get in and do harm to the communications staff on duty. We worked on it and found the money to purchase and install an electric door lock. This was a stop gap measure, until we could purchase a whole new door and frame with interior, desk mounted, electronic locking/unlocking system. I came to the office one morning shortly thereafter, and guess what, we were targeted again. Rather, the Chief was, for "locking the door to the police department so victims could not get in to talk to the police". The short and acre wide female doing the complaining, had been sent in it turns out, was supposedly mad that she had lost her pager and came to the police department to find it, but could not get in. This tail of tragedy only grew and grew until women were being raped on the front lawn of the police station because they could not get in to the station. It really got bizarre. The facts that the dispatcher would open the door and that a patrol unit was only a minute or so away, and that the city had a responsibility to protect its employees, made no difference. Over and over again, I saw the good citizens who privately voiced outrage for conduct of the minority, yet those same ones, who could have helped lead the city, refused to step up and wrest the controls away from the radicals bent on regressive destruction. Fear of retribution was present, that is true. Lord knows I had been the most frequent target, so I understood that, but I could not agree with mindset. If you don't like it, step up to the plate. It was not to be.

The Federal investigation was basically over. The indictments were being prepared and the testimony was being presented to the Grand Jury. I even wrote a letter to the U.S. Attorney in Houston requesting that even the lowest or most insignificant violation against all of the officers be indicted and prosecuted, as that was the only sure way to rid the agency and city of these parasites and criminal violators. I even broached the possibility of filing a RICO violation against the city and the department, so that the government could step in and wipe the whole slate clean. I even had made some preliminary arrangements for city police protection with outside agencies, in the event that everyone of my personnel were put on the block. It would have been tough, expensive and a real pain in the backside, but talk about turning a corner. What a wake up call that would have been.

Then came the next attack. Mostly aimed at myself. By this time, I had packed up my wife and moved her to San Antonio as the heat level had just gotten to high and I did not want her in harms way. So I was living alone, physically, but there was her and many others who I knew were supporting me. One of them was the ASAC for the FBI in McAllen. He told me one day on his mobile phone that "we need someone like you there, so hang in there". I know he meant it, but...

The collective charge came with a barrage of accusations, falsified affidavits and allegations from personnel that were so awkwardly configured that it would have been evident to anyone with half a brain that it was a set up, but the media and others were buying in. The DA office was ask twice by the city manager to investigate the allegations and he declined, stating, "there is nothing to it and I am not getting involved in the small town political issues surrounding this mess". That was stated to the city attorney by the District Attorney and then to me. We needed someone from the outside, with credibility, to look at the allegations and then, upon conclusion, deposit them in the circular file, where they deserved to be from the outset. I had supposedly assaulted and choked two officers, stole city funds, bought ,and used cocaine, interfered with an investigation, destroyed evidence and more. It was laughable, but stupidly believed.

Finally, the DA, motivated by politics that he previously wanted to avoid, sent his henchmen to "investigate". I knew then, it was only a matter of time and that the truth would be a victim on the funeral pire for lawful law enforcement. True to nature, the investigation was cockeyed to say the least. The city manager wholeheartedly agreed, but he was in the cooker too and trying to apply a salve as quick as he could. Whenever I want to get mad or have a good laugh, I go to the box with the falsified affidavits in it. The imperfections in the information, the physical makeup of the documents and the process of preparing them was so amateurish as to defy belief, but even the so called legal beagles from the DA's office refused to look at and even acknowledge the facts. It was politically and monetarily time for the reformist Chief to go.

We, and I mean we, the city manager, the Mayor, Mrs. Villegas, Mr. Hernandez and others, had made a difference. Maybe, it was not a long lasting difference, but a difference and one for the good. We came close to completing what we set out to do, but then close only counts in horse-shoes and hand grenades. Ha?

Robert was trying to save his job. Hell, like me, he needed it. David was really nervous about what was coming, but was also looking for a way to sustain himself in the face of a coming new power to the city council. As fate would have it, on the very day that I finished compiling and typing and arranging all of the documents required of the system, to finally dispose of the remaining crooked personnel in the department, Robert called and wanted to talk. One thing that I had done, knowing how people can turned to quick sand, was to maintain a daily and running account of all the actions and information within the department, my office, the city and whatever else affected them. It is an extensive record brought on by the lessons of the past. It tells it all, only trouble is, in the years to come, no one gives a damn. There would be no cheers of Gerringer for President. There would be a few thank you from some area officers, administrators, and local citizens, but like fame, doing good work, is fleeting and memories are short.

I took a legal box with me containing the documents and evidence on over twenty-seven criminal violations committed by the remainder of the original force of personnel and drove over to meet with Robert. The goal, after almost eleven months, and damn hard work, had finally gotten to within view of reality. It would be for Robert and David to review them, share them with the Mayor and others of suitable station, and then drop a net on the whole bunch. The fastest way to rid the city of the corrupt influence within the department was to do so administratively and then let the courts do the rest, if they would. It was not to be. We were not to be. The old rule was returning and no one, outside of myself, wanted to stand up in front of the stampede.

We had a long discussion and Robert was dejected, but still trying to salvage his job. There is a long record of this meeting and what was said, so in the end there is no dispute as to what was said and done. I liked Robert from the beginning, I did the whole way through, and even though he gave up his milk in the end, I still like the man. In fact, in 1999, as another civil suit ravaged the city due to a police officer sexually violating a female prisoner, Robert was deposed. During that deposition, Robert again stated that at the time and even now, Gerringer was the man that was needed and could have cleaned out the department and made it into a good one. So, with nothing to gain, at that late date, that told me and the attorneys that what had been undertaken and accomplished was right and good and respected. It just was not politically correct.

Robert admitted that the goal was at hand, that the investigation of myself was bogus, and that the lawsuit was nothing more than a grab for money, but the political wind had put him in a position of having other things to deal with. We ultimately agreed that I would resign and accept four months of severance pay and we would go on. I hated leaving a job undone, especially one that I had been mandated to perform by those that had appointed me, but I loaded up, and headed north. My wife was happy as a bug in a new rug. What did the future hold for us now? Whatever it was, we would come through it and be the stronger for the adversity of the last few years.

The fur flew within just a few months. The election went as I had come to suspicion. The two radical types won and the Mayor lost control of the direction of events. Robert and David were both fired. There were officers who we had succeeded in getting shed of that were brought back. The new Chief was cut from the same bolt of cloth as those we were trying to get rid of. In fact, he had been on suspension for years under investigation for various narcotics and other theft related offenses. But, that is what the idiots wanted, and that is what they got. The Federal Grand Jury returned the indictments. Clemente and six others went to prison. The media beat their chest about the corruption in Donna and that something has to be done. How quickly they change their collective tunes. Since late 1977 more officers have been caught up in criminal conduct. More investigations have been pursued. The DEA agent in charge of the case moved to San Antonio. The DPS narcotics case officer was promoted to Ranger. The position of city manager has been filled and vacated on about three or four subsequent occasions. The new mayor has been indicted for assaulting a lawyer in a sports bar in Donna and the Donna PD continues its same old ways. The more things change, the more they stay the same and Donna is doomed as long its good citizens continue to sit back and let the corrupt and self-serving control what does and does not get done. Oh, the water sytem, it is still screwed up and residents still get free water and sewer.

Weeds will grow even in the most well cultivated soil.

The Author

CHAPTER NINE

THE FROZEN NORTH

One of my favorite movies is North To Alaska, with that rugged and patriotic star, The Duke, Mr. John Wayne. Having viewed in magazines, on television and in movies the breathe taking scenery of that seemingly pristine and expansive land, I had often thought about going to Alaska to visit. To view a land where there are areas that have never seen or felt the trod of a human foot. The mountains majesty, the clear and cold waters teeming with fish, snow and ice deeper than a polar bear is tall and views of touched beauty. A frontier, even in the twenty-first century, where you can see Grizzly Bears, Caribou, Polar Bears, Snow Fox and many other species. So, you think about it, but you cannot ever really afford to get any closer than you will by watching the Discovery Channel.

After having departed the den of viperous souls in Donna, I languished between positions. Even with twenty-seven years in the business, I was over fifty and having placed more than a few officers in prison, getting another position was proving to be tougher than expected. Since about 1975 I had been a pocket watch collector and had studied the ins and outs of how to take the various types and makes apart and to repair them. It was a hobby which relieved the stresses of a more pressurized professional life. Not to mention that you can make a little income in the business. So, I opened a shop in my home and went to buying, selling, trading and repairing pocket watches to help pay the bills. I had acquired the largest collection of watches made by The Manistee Watch Company, numbering twenty-two, and there were less than fifty known to exist in the United States. In between sending out resumes, that is how I helped my beautiful wife keep us afloat. A good part of my dealings were on the internet, specifically that auction site named eBay. It was through this auction site that I met and became friends with a man from Alaska. St. Mary's, Alaska to be exact. I had to go buy a map of Alaska to find it, because it damn sure isn't on any beaten path. In fact, you damn near cannot get there from here, or from anywhere. Walton was the city manager of the city and in our almost daily exchanges of emails, we became very friendly and open. Walton is an intellectual type, with a very rough exterior and with no compunction towards being reserved, especially in his verbalization of opinions. Anyway, he came to know some of my background and I his. Part of that knowledge was the fact that I was a law enforcement officer and a Chief of Police.

As it turns out, the City of St. Mary's had its own department of public safety, which was responsible for the provision of police, fire, communications, ems, and detention facilities to a native American population of Yupiks. The city had a population of about five hundred and covered over two hundred and fifty square miles of frozen tundra. It was physically located at the juncture of the Yukon and Andreasfsky Rivers, about eighty miles inland from the Bering Sea and about 150 miles south of the Artic Circle. It was a damn cold and isolated land, on the edge of the hills and ultimately the mountains, and the great expanse of the marsh like tundra. It is way the hell out in the middle of nowhere. In fact you are closer to Russia than you are Anchorage. During the ensuing months of selling watches to Walton and providing him with all kinds of information about other watches that he had it came to light that the city was shortly going to be in need of a Director of Public Safety to oversee operations. Being out of a job, we soon came to an agreement, I would come up on a contract for three months and serve as the interim Director (Chief) and then the city would pay my way home. Hey, it was a job, at least for three months, an income to help pay the bills, and I would get to see a land that I had not seen before. Sign me up coach…and on May 22, 1999, it was wheels up from San Antonio International Airport. The route would take me from San Antonio to Denver, changing planes and on to Seattle and then Anchorage. Now in Anchorage I would catch a Penn Air flight for St. Mary's. My wife did not cotton to such an expanse of distance separating us, but she knew I needed to work and we did need the money. Besides, what the hell kind of trouble could I get in to way up there, in the middle of no where? My wife did tell me, NO rubbing noses with any indigenous females. I took no suits, no nice boots or any other creature comforts as Walton told me there was no need for them and the weight limit on the plane reduced what you could bring in. My housing was to be upstairs from an old fish processing plant and was free. So, except for food, it was a free and paying job. Little did I know, again.

The flight to St. Mary's was about two and a half hours and most of the time you could not see anything for all the clouds, but when they opened up, it was all frozen, covered with ice and snow, and resembling a lumpy pool table. There was nothing out there. Yet, it was damn sure pretty. On approach to St. Mary's you could see the city, nestled amongst some low hills on the bank of the Andreafsky River. It was quaint, 19th century in some respects and damn sure cold. The airport is actually a collection of scattered buildings and a long gravel runway running east and west. The landing, well let's just say we got down in one piece. On opening the door to the plane if there was any idea of being in a tropical clime, it was quickly, no instantly, dispelled by a blast of frigidly cold air. I do mean a blast. It was like being in a vacuum and suddenly someone threw a switch and filled the space with gaseous nitrogen. Damn it was cold. Stepping off the aircraft was like stepping back in time, way back in time. The "terminal" was a small wood and metal frame building. The baggage claim area was a big metal container, open on one side, and moved around by a big fork lift. The ground crew, ha ha, would take the baggage, boxes, duffles, mail sacks, shrink wrapped containers and other stuff out of the belly of the plane, throw it in the container and then the fork lift would pick it all up and set it down between the gate to the tarmac and the parking area. From there you fended for yourself, rain, snow or shine. Standing next to a an old four wheel drive with lights on top, was a tall man I took for the Chief. Next to him was a throw back to Grizzly Adams, beard and all. That had to be Walton. We introduced ourselves, and retrieved my suitcases from the container, loaded them in the Chief's vehicle and headed for town. On the way in, I got a quick sightseeing tour of part of my jurisdiction. The landfill and noctural feeding ground of more than a few brown and black bears, the road down to a seasonal fish camp on the Yukon, the rutted road down to another Eskimo village also sitting on the Yukon and a short story about the area. It was wild, in every sense of the word. Six and half miles later, we arrived in St. Mary's proper. It was close to something out of a picture post card and yes, primitive, by any standards of the lower forty-eight. Some of the scenery was really beautiful. Some of the "residences" were pitiful. How in the hell did they manage to keep from freezing to death? I found out later, that not all of them did. Now, the first thought was, there would be damn little to do in terms of law enforcement up here, it was just too blasted cold to be getting into mischief, of any kind. How quickly I had forgotten, humans live here, and that means trouble.

My quarters were indeed upstairs. I hauled my bags up and took a quick survey of the eminities available. There were a number of rooms for sleeping, a big kitchen area with a refrigerator, stove and cabinets, a table to eat at, two couches and a television. Of course, it only got one channel, but that was to be expected way the heck out here. Limm, the Chief, came back by and picked me up and we started the transition and getting acquainted routine. Damn nice guy, he was just fed up with living out in the toolies and was taking a job in Ketchikan with a trading post. Yep, a trading post. These stores were sell all affairs and had been started way back in the 1800's when white men first started showing their ugly mugs in the region. Everything that came to the stores for sell, or to the city in general, came by either barge, when the rivers were not frozen, or it was flown in. Now you could take a dog sled or snowmobile, depending on the time of the year, and go overland for about 115 miles to Bethel, but it was a bitch of a trip and no guarantee you would get there or back without losing your way or toes and fingers. Telephone calls were by satellite, as was television reception. Beyond that, the rest of the world just might as well not have existed. There was no place to go. The big past time, in the non-frozen period, was fishing. The endless miles of rivers was a fisherman's paradise.

City hall was a one story and long narrow building which double as a community center and council hall. It sat on a pier and beam foundation, which was slipping down the hill. The police station was located up the hill and was basically a one room affair attached to a large garage which housed the cities one pumper fire truck and an ambulance. It was heated around the clock to insure that the units would start. The department had three vehicles, all of which had seen better days, and were held together by spit and bailing wire. The detention facility was two home made cells with steel doors and wooden bars to keep them locked in place. Limm gave me a tour of the city and pointed out all of the houses and named off who lived where. There was a short course in the types of crime that would be experienced and a quick run down on the legal system and statutes of the State of Alaska. The department had two officers, Tom and Clay. Tom was the Sergeant, although there was no need for a Sergeant, and Clay was the newest, except for me. Both seemed knowledgible and affable. I then went up to city hall and met with the city manager and was introduced to his three staff and then we took another tour of the city. It was a revealing meeting, as I learned about some of the Yupik traditions, culture, and ways of doing things and the way that they thought. It was obvious, Walton had been in the sticks too long, but like he said, he probably could not get along back in civilization.

There was also an Alaska State Trooper outpost located in St. Mary's. The State of Alaska paid about $1500 a month for a small office space located in a small apartment complex for the two troopers and also paid for their living quarters. The two troopers were Dave and Jane. Jane was a redhead and someone you could depend on come hell or high water. Each of the two troopers were responsible for overseeing law enforcement in about fifteen to twenty villages each. They would generally fly from one to the other when they had calls or cases to work in those villages. The law enforcement presence in rural Alaska came in various versions. First there were the Tribal police. They were appointed by who ever was in power in a particular village at the time. They had no training, no resources to speak of, and nearly all had their darker side. Then there were the village police who were also untrained and basically appointed the same way. They both did pretty much what they wanted to and it was not so much of a position of law enforcement as it was a pay check. Both would generally call the State Troopers if they had a problem. Then there was the VPSO's or Village Public Safety Officers's, which were under the direct control, so to speak, of the Alaska State Troopers. These individuals would go to the Trooper Academy for a couple of weeks, the same as the regular certified police candidates, but then would return to the bush. Regular officers would have to graduate and be certified. There was a saying in the bush that yesterdays crook was today's VPSO. The system, in my humble opinion, was a flaming joke. Then you had sworn and certified officers. Too damn few and far between and poorly paid and equipped, to say the least. I soon discovered that, for the general population, police were no more respected in the bush, than they were in the lower forty-eight. In fact, I cam to see that Eskimos probably disliked the police even more than other humanoids did. In fact, the only thing that Ekimos really liked were the government checks that came like clockwork every month.

At my first meeting with the two officers I kept it light and simple. I was only there for three months and was not going to get worked up over anything or get immersed in any major problems. There was just not time. Foolish boy! We talked in general, and I complimented them on their work and the hardships of their locations and dedication. I did tell them both, that we would get along great, but that they did need to know that the only time we would get cross ways was if one of the became involved in any type of criminal conduct. That was my one main rule, you wear a badge, don't violate it. Now, at the outset, I believed it was safe, for what could anyone get into way out there. Again, I had forgotten, there were other humans here, and that was all that was necessary. Why me Lord?

Well, I will tell you up front, one of the two officers must have not taken my warning seriously. For the first three months of my "tour" it was a learning process, an education in human nature, and a study in how the "system" does not work for everyone. The DA office was located in Bethel, Alaska, one hundred and twelve air miles away. If you arrest someone, you take them to a magistrate, which we had one of in St. Mary's, or at least that was what he was paid for, and then you lock them up in our cells and wait for the next plane going to Bethel. You would escort the prisoner to Bethel and turn him, or her, over to a State Trooper. If you had time, you could hitch a ride in to downtown Bethel and get a hot meal, go to the store, rent a movie, buy something, anything, to take home, get a haircut (a major item), and then hustle back to the airport to fly back to St. Mary's. Hopefully, all in one day. The heading was 132 degrees. Just in case you went down. Oh, did I mention that there are more small plane crashes in Alaska than anywhere else in the entire United States?

Yes Alice, there is crime in Alaska. Even in the bush of Alaska. For the first three months, we ran over one hundred calls per month. Now that is not much compared to nearly any city of any size in the lower forty-eight, but in this neck of the woods, it seemed like an enormous amount. Violations centered around the use and abuse of drugs, mostly marijuana, and alcohol. I said centered around, but not limited to just those substances.

There are thefts, burglaries, stolen vehicles (even though there is no where out there to drive one to), drug possession and smuggling, sexual offenses by the truck load, alcohol smuggling, robbery and the like. What is funny, is that for most offenses, police are used to the perpetrator taking off and trying to go somewhere. In the frozen north, there is actually, no where to go. Steal a car and drive up and down the very few miles of road surface and then get caught. Rob the store or steal from a residence, how do you get away? The answer is, the police go to the airport and wait on you to show up or they quickly identify you and go to your house and get you. The phrase you can run, but you can't hide, takes on a new meaning up there. In St. Mary's it was illegal to transport alcohol in to the city limits and it was illegal to manufacture alcohol. Yet, once you got it there, it was not illegal to be drunk in public, or to possess or consume alcohol. Selling alcohol was also illegal, but damn near everyone was in to it. For example, if you take a trip to Anchorage, you would go to the liquor store and buy as many plastic bottles of gin or vodka as you could stuff in to your suitcase or a box and then put it on the plane and bring it home. The cost of a roundtrip ticket to the city was about $400. In St. Mary's it was not unusual to sell one small bottle of booze for $100. So you can see how the travelers would pay for their trips to town. It was a constant problem and many a booze case was made at the airport. All you had to do was stand there and look at them (the deplaning passengers) and who did not go near their luggage or boxes and you could figure out which contained the booze. I can't remember how many bottles we poured down the drain, but it was a bunch. Of course, it was a good service, as the alcohol helped keep the pipes open. But, seizing the booze sure made the locals upset. It was a cottage industry. There were a few villages that took their desires to keep booze out of the villages so serious that the village officials would even have you strip at the airport. Like everywhere else, even in the native American communities, there was a push by some Eskimos to stop the adverse influences of alcohol upon Eskimos, but for the most part it is a lot of talk and foot stamping tirades at government, but when push comes to shove, the booze flows on. I do agree with those ardent few though, alcohol is the yoke of despair for the Eskimos, just like for the Souix and other Indian nations. It is not a problem that is going to be eliminated. Mainly because, humans will be humans and the amount of money to be made is just out of sight. The smugglers and sellers are not limited to the "white man" either, there are many Eskimos who sell the mixtures to their own. Like any other race, ethnicity or culture, there are good people, so so people, and then there are the dregs, scam artist and crooks that prey on anyone for money.

The land is beautiful, wild and mostly untamed. There is a lot of things to see and do, in the wilderness vein, but if you are looking for the more recognized creature comforts of the lower states, you can almost forget it. There was only one television channel available in my digs, and most of the time it was a giant bore. More channels came in via satellite, but the cost was too high and the city would not spring for it. Radio was there, but the atmosphere played hell with it most of the time or the airwaves were filled with local type news of no interest to me. The two trading post stores had just about anything you wanted or they could order it for you from a catalog, but the prices got pretty rich, mainly because of the transportation costs. I like to go up on top of cemetery hill, as it was called, and sit there in the morning or evening and watch the sun, or the moon, depending on what time of year it was. It was a beautiful site. On several occasions Walton took me in his boat, up the Andeafsky River to fish. On those sojourns I caught a few scrappy fish, but enjoyed more looking at the scenery. I saw Moose, beaver, fish of course, bears, the magnificent American Bald Eagle and other critters. I took a bucket full of pictures and sent them home. I wanted to go further up the river or to near Nome and pan for gold, but there just was not enough time. This is a land that everyone should be proud of. It provides a cultural living for the Eskimos and the potential for others to enjoy things not often seen. The oil that exists up and under the North Slope is stated to be massive. That supply would be a boon to our economy and that of the Eskimos. It just has to be accomplished in the best manner, for all concerned.

For a young buck, one with the drives of most "normal" people, if you know what I mean, it can be a lonely existence. The lack of female companionship wears on some more than others. That seems to have been the main point of trouble for the Sergeant. Walton verbalized his concerns to me. I received little unsubstantiated tidbits of information from citizens, but nothing you could hang your hat on. At the same time I had to understand that some there did not like the man, while others did. So there could be other motivations for grousing. I quietly compiled information and undertook an inquiry to see if there might be any thing that would substantive. By the fifth month, I got the answer. Not necessarily the one I wanted, but an answer.

There were a lot of complaints about the prosecution system in the bush, and more particularly the lax attitude of the prosecutors towards the felony cases that law enforcement developed. In particular, my agency had received information that a very large quantity of booze would be smuggled in by boat. The trip down the Yukon would take several hours, but I parked myself up on the hill overlooking the river and the docking area and waited. I told Clay to get some sleep, but to leave his radio on in case I called. Well, sure enough about 4 am, here came a big boat, as described, down to the registration and name, hauling rear up the river and right to the bank in town. Clay hustled down and along the bank and got close enough to verify the previously provided information. Two of the occupants of the boat were now asleep. We could see a pile of alcohol in the boat, so we woke them up and did our thing. We got the aid of Jane from the Troopers and the work commenced. This was a big haul, not just in booze, but in the money it represented when sold in the villages. We seized the booze, the boat, a shotgun and miscellaneous stuff and placed the culprits in jail. All the paper work was done and sent to the DA. It was a damn good and clean case. Yet, the DA decided to dismiss it. Well, I got irritated, to say the least, and began making calls. The city manager got in the act, as well as the Mayor. Before it was all over, the DA re-filed the case and St. Mary's was to receive a visit from the Colonel of the Troopers, the

Commissioner and a couple of others. We woke up the politicians. During this fill their ears meeting, the Colonel and I met and discussed the Sergeant problem. It seems that the Sergeant had admitted in a couple of polygraph sessions, taken for other positions, that he was in to possession of child pornography. Bingo!!! With that conversation came a friendly exchange, but one that let the Colonel know that I was not pleased by being kept in the dark. He apologized and we went on. Of course, the rub came again as a popinjay Trooper who was running the case, still did not want to get along. We had words and this old man set him straight. We executed a search warrant on the Sergeant's apartment, and found a bunch of very nasty evidence. He was cooked. I explained the situation to him and he wrote out his resignation. Afterwards, I ask him, "why in the hell did you do this?" His limp reply was that he was way out here, away from his fiancé, and with no physical companionship and it was a way to vent. Well, porno is a damn big problem and makes many a ton of money every year, but that had to be a damn poor excuse. Of course, I learned that there were others within the community that had "strange" viewing habits and most of it came via the mail or the internet. Of course, the last I heard was the case was going no where. I disagreed with the tactic and source of the Trooper information acquisition, but not with the taking to task of an officer who was engaged in a conduct that was beyond the pale. I went back later with Jane and arrested him and we transported him to Bethel. The even dumber part is, on our first meeting, I had pointedly told him and Clay, not to engage in any illegal conduct because I would have no sympathy for them if they did. Plain English and a bold black warning apparently went unheeded.

For the next few months, Clay and I worked about a hundred hours a week, each. Fortunately, the stringent exercise of the law, in the past few months, had driven home the realization that the law was here and not to be trifled with, so in the last two and a half months in St. Mary's, calls dwindled down to zero.

On the day that I flew out of St. Mary's, for the last time, I hope, the temperature was –30 degrees with a light snow, and that did not include the wind chill factor. Damn it was cold. I hated to leave Clay there alone, but my time was up and admittedly, I was glad to be leaving a bleak existence. Clay hated to see me leave also, but he had grown and learned and I knew he could handle himself. Besides he could always call on Jane until the city hired someone else. On top of that, the citizens were in a much more compliant mood and, hopefully, it would hold. I worry too about Walton, as his health was not all that great, and from what I understood, he had no one else or any where else to go. To this date I think about him and hope he is well. Clay ultimately left St. Mary's and went to the North Slope to work temporarily and at last word was now in Michigan going back to school.

The seven months in the far reaches of Alaska was a multi-faceted education, to say the least. I appreciated the opportunity to serve the citizens of that area and for the high praise that I received from the Mayor for my leadership and work, the friendship of Clay, the friendship of Walton and the exposure to another culture and world of ideas. Yet, I was glad to be out. I flew back to Texas, and it took eighteen hours, and to this day, I still can see in my mind's eye, some of the most beautiful country God ever made. Frozen over most of the time, I miss it to a degree, but then I get a shiver and that missing fades to reality.

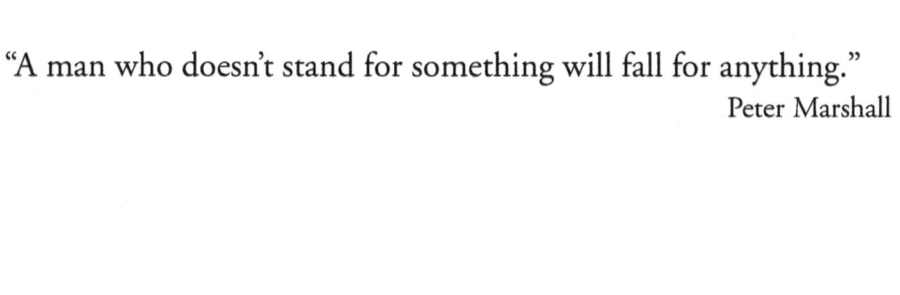

"A man who doesn't stand for something will fall for anything."

Peter Marshall

CHAPTER TEN

WHERE AND WHAT NOW

Fuel has been added to the fire. As I sit here in my cubby hole, writing on this exercise in frustration relief, along comes the news that an FBI Special Agent has been arrested and jailed on treasonist charges. It seems that this agent, who is not the first by the way, regardless of what the Bureau's spin doctors will say, has been working for the the KGB, and its post-Communist successors, of the Soviet Union, now the Russian Federated States, since 1985. The agent has sold an inestimatable amount of national secret information to our adversaries. The agent used dead drops, encryption devices and other means of delivering classified information to the Soviets/Russians. Of course, several questions arise. Can the FBI, as an agency, legitimately claim they are the best in the nation? Can the FBI continue to lay claim to the high morale ground in the law enforcement profession? Why did it take fifteen years to catch their own agent? Where was the counterintelligence system that the FBI is charged with in the United States? I could ask a lot more, but the main point is, the FBI, like every other agency, has its corrupt personnel. Whether they are in to narcotics, theft, selling secrets, or whatever, they are no better or worse than the rest.

Like was stated earlier in this work, corruption comes in many forms. You can run a full field background investigation on everybody concerning everything, from day one to the present and you can bestow security clearances and procedures until they blot out the sun, but you cannot and never will be able to eliminate corruption.

Hell, the three big boys on the block, the CIA, FBI, and NSA have all had corrupt personnel, dopers, thieves and traitors in their ranks. I guess one thing that really rankles many on the lower levels, is the arrogant and know it all attitudes of the big boys, especially when they are in contact with the little boys. The feds don't trust the locals cause they are not "cleared" and may be in to some type of corrupt conduct. The locals don't trust the feds, cause they have a cob up their ass, believe they are better than the locals and are not bashful about not trusting the locals. Yet, neither the big boys nor the little boys can claim purity. All try to hide the fact that corruption may exist. All play the game of media smoozing to try and put the best face on the situation. Some are more adept at stifling access to information that would make them look bad, the FBI in particular, and that adds to the resentment on various levels. So, what the heck do we do?

There are no quick fixes and no certain answers, but there are some points that we as a profession and more importantly, we as a society must undertake to adopt, internalize and profess publicly, if we are to turn this dark horse around. First and foremost, WE HAVE TO RETURN TO TELLING THE TRUTH, and nothing but the truth, no matter what. We will never achieve the utopian state of total truth telling, but we can strive to return to a time, when telling the truth took precedence over politically correct semantics and other verbal manipulations. We cannot raise our children, and expose them on a daily basis to lies, distortions, untruth, personal expedience and all of the other tawdry methodologies in use in this day and time, without them learning that to engage in such conduct is beneficial and personally rewarding. They and their children must come to grips with the fact that responsibility and accountability are not out distanced by privileges and position.

Bottom line is, we have to re-capture a higher morale ground, and defend it against all comers. No, you cannot legislate morals and I do not suggest that, but we have to cast off the malaise that has gripped us, ie. William Jefferson Clinton and wife syndrome, and return to, or advance to, a time when the majority of people believed in the rule of law, in authority, in right and wrong, in God, in Country and in Duty. No you don't have to be a religious rightist to be moral and upright, you just have to be more than a self-centered, money grubbing, anything goes type of individual.

Second, we have got to find a method by which we can reduce, in far greater numbers and percentages, the level of criminal violations within our nation. To say that violent crime is down this year as compared to the last five years, when the last five years was greater that the preceeding ten years, is nothing more than a play on words and a manipulation of the numbers. Crime continues to rise, across the board, no matter whose statistics you read. Why? Mainly, because of two points. One is the oceanic flood of narcotics on our streets, in our schools, in our homes, in our offices, in our government buildings, in our agencies of government, amongst the police, the teachers, the doctors, the attorneys, the engineers and damn near everyone else. It is an epidemic. Another point is that there is no fear of punishment.

We are, and have been for close to thirty years, in a creeping mindset of political correctness, of alibi construction, blame shifting and excuse manufacturing. More and more groups and individuals design and hoist onto the mantel of consciousness all types and manners of "reasons" why black is not white, right is wrong, wrong is acceptable in these circumstances and it is societies fault. For ages to come people will remember but pay less and less heed to the prophetic words of former President Clinton, "it all depends on what the definition of is, is". How stupid and apologetic we have become. Criminals do not fear punishment, as punishment is passé. In not fearing punishment, in not being held accountable, far too many have received the signal that "acting out" is correct behavior, especially if you can create a new phrase or ism or syndrome to explain away to a gullible society why your conduct was appropriate.

I recall the time when I was the Agent-in-Charge of the U.S. Marshals office in Del Rio. We covered a stretch of territory bigger than most cities and close to the size of some states. At the same time I was an officer in the National Association of Deputy U.S. Marshals, which had as a primary goal, the improvement of training, hiring, employment recognition, benefits and more. As the editor of the newsletter I would sometimes pen an admittedly caustic piece to try and get the powers that be, at the time, to sit up and pay attention to the problems faced in the field. One of those problems was that well qualified personnel could not obtain promotions if they were not a member of the controlling clique. That was wrong headed and self-defeating to the agency. On one occasion I wrote, " you cannot achieve advancement without having learned to maintain a permanent pucker at chair seat level". Well, that got some attention in D.C. and they sent down word through a friend of mine in the Border Patrol, that I should be more reserved in my comments as they would not like to see me hurt my career. The message was clear, shut up or else. The next issue hit where they had left off.

You say, but you are disrespectful, so why should anyone want to promote you or listen to you. To such a comment I reply, respect is a two way street. You have to earn respect. It is not bestowed with the job, regardless of the level. Oh, sure, we all are due a degree of respect because we are humans and we should be civil to each other, but there are those upon whom that idea is a vacant lot. You earn my respect by treating me as a professional, even an equal, not by talking down, trying to intimidate, force to prostitute myself, or to commit an act that is against the rules. I earn your respect by doing my duty to the utmost of my capability, by being honest in word and deed and by following the precepts of the office and profession. To do otherwise would earn me disrespect and deservedly so. Yet, they are many who believe they walk on water, do not expel noxious odors and know everything there is to know about anything. They treat personnel with arrogance, disdain and distrust. That mentality spreads and is a corrosive of the most nasty order.

Politicians are among the numbers of those who are most adept at being jerks, liars and influence peddlers. In fact politics, and its purveyors and wannabes, have ruined many a good law enforcement agency, operation and individuals. All for personal, family, friend or advantage reasons, none of which were in step with the goals, methods, operations and desires of those ultimately affected.

So where do we go from here? How will we get there? Who will set the standards and guide the way? Do we need to go anywhere? Do we need a different standard? Do we really need someone to take us or to guide us there? These are legitimate questions of worth. They all have an answer. Not the answer of some desk bound yuppized ivy leaguer, but an answer from within each of us, individually and collectively. Will we all arrive at the same answer? Not in this world! Will we all agree with the answer of the other? Wrong again! Yet, if the majority reach the same answer, do we accept it as ours? Do we accept it only if it is the answer we wanted? Do we rebel and act out if the answer of the majority is not the one we wanted? Do we take any action against those in the minority who do not agree with the answer? Well, the answers are clear........to each of us in our own way of thinking and believing and that is where the rub comes in.

Do we go back and relive the past? No. Do we go forward? Yes. Do we go forward without being conscious of the past? Better not. Do we ignore the lessons of the past? Hope not. Can we go forward without leaning on the past? Possibly, but if we fail to learn from the past, are we not doomed to repeat it?

In the end, the ultimate answer lies within each of us and each of us must rely upon the hope that the ability to discern appropriate answers lies within each of us.

It can get damn confusing.

You will surely reap that which you sow.

The Author

Chapter Eleven

Waxing Philosophically

When in college, one of the courses that I liked the most was Philosophy. It was mentally intriguing and challenging. Granted, I am no Socrates, Aristole or Plato, but reading their works and digesting their ideas, cannot but help to stimulate the juices of thought. Employing some of the tenets of philosophy to the theme of this work seems most appropriate.

What is the theme of this work you ask? Maybe, if you have to ask, you have not and will not have read this far in to the book, maybe you do not and will not grasp what I am trying to point out. Then, on the other hand, maybe I have failed to make a bright line of understanding. I do not believe so, but the theme herein is public corruption, which exhibits itself in many forms, characters, acts and omissions.

As a law enforcement professional, I have mostly spoken about public corruption in that somewhat narrow venue, but it is definitely not confined to that theatre. As for the police, they do many of the same things that others do, including the crooks. One of the worst is that they rationalize their illicit, unethical and unprofessional behavior. The cop on the beat, who is on the take, or shaking down crooks, running dope or any other such conduct, does not see himself as a crook, even though he does not want to get caught. The officer will rationalize to him/herself that such money making endeavors are, at least, to be tolerated, because the pay is too low, or I worked damn hard for nothing, or the city owes it too me, or I am a police officer and they won't catch me, or any one of a few hundred other such flimsy excuses. This rationalization begins with the commission of the first, and more often than not, a very minor transgression. For example, taking a packet of gum from a store without paying for it, whether the owner knows or not. The officer might say, I protect him all night from the robbers and thieves, he owes it too me, or he won't miss it, or I buy enough in here I deserve it, or he makes a hell of a lot more than I do, so he won't miss it type excuses—rationales. From there, it can easily grow and become a major problem. This is the gradual erosion process that eats away at the will, the oath, the integrity and the ethics of the individual. If the individual had any of those commendable traits to begin with. Yet, with each growing incident, the rationalization process grows in proportion, until it has reached the point that the individual fully, consciously and rationally believes that the concoction of rationales has indeed given legitimacy to the actions. The cops don't look at themselves as criminals committing crimes, this is only a part of their self-instilled mental program of entitlement(s). They rely on the code of blue silence, on their unshakeable belief that they are too smart to get caught and that society owes me mindsets.

There was a Sergeant in the city where I was the Chief that was of the unabashed opinion that "I am a police officer, I should not be investigated because I wear a badge", and he believed that. Little did he know, I did not, but he would learn. In point of fact, bad cops, even bad public officials in general, do not respect the law, the badge or their office, the oath they swore to or even the community, which they are suppose to represent. The only thing they do respect is fear, mostly fear of getting caught, and the almighty dollars, which they cram in to their bottomless pockets.

When one sees or learns of another who is involved in such conduct, and nothing adverse takes place, that individual may very possibly turn to the view that if he can do it, and get away with it, so can I. There comes the influence of a peer upon a another peer, both of whom are weak to begin with. This influencing factor is a deteriorating one, and has set up a seemingly indestructible ethical and moral decay, that is nibbling away at the foundation of our democracy.

Police, in general, generally complain mightily about the bar associations and its members, that is lawyers and their groups, not the tequila tossing joints. Police believe, and to a point correctly so, that the legal profession is more corrupt than any other. A few years back a study stated that there were more attorneys in prison than police officers and if true, it would support the complaints. Police also believe that the bar associations are so "tight" that they will not discipline their members for wrongful conduct. Again, the perception, at least, is that this is true. However, the police, in one sense, have no right to complain. Rarely, unless truly cornered and forced to, will another officer speak out against a fellow officer. The unions or police associations are not there so much to ferret out bad cops or to support clean agencies and conduct, as they are there to foster their own personal goals and ambitions for power. The same comparisons can be drawn for judges, doctors, dentists, engineers, politicians (unless it is election time or the offending person is of the opposite party), school teachers, professors and yes, even preachers.

Are we, as I believe, moving closer and closer, as a nation and society, toward social democracy? Have we transited from being a nation founded and constructed of integrity and community being, to one of having to be politically correct in what we do instead of being right in what we do? How many of you have seen individuals employed in levels off the ground because of who they knew, what gender they were, what aberrant sexual orientation they held or what the color of their skin was, rather than whether they knew the work, had the qualifications, were a leader or any of the other traits that we have all supposedly been told are what to seek?

All of us have at one time or another. For some it was very up close and personal and thus it had a direct impact. For others, there was no immediate direct impact so they did not concern themselves, but the wave has spread. Will it ever hit the shore and disperse in to the sands of time, only heaven knows and there is not indication forthcoming from that venue. Of course, there is one point that I do believe and that will probably not change and that is that we cannot depend on or trust the politicians to do what needs to be done to correct this growing apathy, pessimism and they owe it to me mentality. Why? That is easy to answer and the answer is that the politicians, like most everyone else, have concentrated their focus on themselves, on winning the next election, on garnering enough monetary support, on manuvering themselves in to position to achieve a certain seat on a certain committee of influence, of increasing their influence and thus their power base, and more overall, of sustaining themselves in whatever office is attractive at the moment, so they can pursue the other gains. They are thus not really interested in the long term safety, mission, desires, goals, visions and aspirations of the those they serve.

We have become, more and more, a nation, or more accurately, a society of entitlement worshippers and seekers. The handout syndrome of the fat, dumb and lazy has spread its tentacles with unceasing aggression. We have to move away from self and toward community. Away from over self-indulgence and in the direction of reasonable abstinence. We have to take responsibility for our conduct, good or bad, and not continually transfer our responsibilities to others. We should raise and train and discipline our children and not leave it to teachers to do so. We should be responsible for the safety and security of our streets and not leave it just to the police to do so. We should be concerned and introspective of our law enforcement agencies for the police of our communities are our communities and the communities are we, the people. Very early on I made the comment that cities generally get what they pay for or want. If they don't care, they get bad police and agencies. If they do care, they can damn sure clean the ranks and the agency up.

Other elements in the equation of decay within the law enforcement ranks is seen in the fact that we hire lesser qualified individuals, we demand less from the individuals we hire, many who come to the ranks do so only for the job and the pay check that comes with it, the level of pride has sunk, the level of respect has sunk and the level of concern for serving has taken a bad hit. We are, or rather many have become complacent, centered only on self, lack pride in belonging, care nothing of service to fellow man and seek more and more entitlements.

We have, like in Washington D.C., Los Angeles, Chicago, Philadelphia, Austin, Houston, and so many others, lowered the standards of who would be acceptable to employ, in an effort to be more politically correct and ethnically inclusive. Yet, the ultimate results were more police committed crimes and all that goes with that mentality. It was a tough lesson, than even today, many have not learned. Now, I will be the first to state, that having high standards is no guarantee. None at all, but you lessen your chances of getting burned and in the end, reduction of exposure is a high concern, or at least it should be.

As this entitlement mentality has spread and become more engrained, a greater and greater percentage of the work force, not limited to just law enforcement either, has taken on the entitlement mindset. As Judith Bardwick stated in her book, ***Danger in the Comfort Zone***, "where workers have no real incentive to achieve and managers have stopped doing the work of requiring real work", people become lazy and complacent and matter of fact towards their duties and responsibilities. They believe they are owed a job, and a damn good paying job, but they in turn do not have to produce damn good work. That attitude is found in law enforcement. There are officers who do only what they absolutely have to, to get by, and nothing more. The goal then is only personal, money, power and influence, and with the lessening of the ethics and values comes more complacency, more deviant behavior and more of the entitlement mentality. Sadly, many officers who see it, do not care to try and say or do anything to change it or stop it. Even more sadly, is the litany of Chiefs, Sheriffs, Administrators and other managers who are wrapped up more in saving their own destinies and much less concerned about the agency, the community, the profession or even the oath they took. So they close a blind eye, stick their heads in the sand and pray like hell that it will go away or at least not be discovered. Some make it through, but others don't. For those that don't, the blame game becomes the main focus. That is then followed by the inevitable "we're going to fix it" game, but in reality, that idea is bankrupt before it gets started, and anything that comes, is usually superficial and cosmetic. So mediocrity reigns! Who is ultimately to blame? The officer, his supervisor, the commander, the Chief, the Mayor, the City Manager or the citizens? The answer is…all of the above. We have to support our employees when they are right. We have to discipline employees when they are wrong. We have to put employees in jail when they commit illegal acts. The politicians have to support the ones they appoint. The citizens have to support the ones doing right and get rid of the ones doing wrong. That is the way it should work, but don't hold your breathe.

Lt. Ken Adcox of the El Paso Police Department, wrote an article entitled, "Doing Bad Things for Good Reasons", which was published in the January 2000 issue of The Police Chief, which bears on the ethical behavior of police personnel. Lt. Adcox wrote, "Unlawful police behavior can come in many forms, including the use of unacceptable or illegal means to accomplish desired ends. Officers who engage in this type of deviant conduct view it as acceptable police practices when such actions are resorted to in the name of justice. Over time, this behavior may become habitual and once this deviant behavior has become the norm, it is no longer recognized as deviant". Of course, even in law enforcement, nothing happens in a vacuum. Sooner or later, everything will come to light, and for the majority who engage in illicit conduct, the assumption is that it will not. In our nation, as in most others, we applaud, publicly recognize, bestow medals and laud to the highest the physical bravery and courage of law enforcement officers. There are officers who find themselves instantaneously thrown in to situations whereupon their actions result in the saving of a life or other equally significant activity are heroes. That is a correct and appreciated act of recognition. However, what happens to the officer who finds him/herself thrown in to a situation in which they are pulled in to or made aware of conduct by other officials that is illegal, unethical or unprofessional? If that individual upholds the rule of law and the oath that was sworn, and reveals the conduct to superiors, government leaders and/or the citizens, does her or she receive the same hero status recognition? Seldom! In fact, such individuals are generally looked upon as traitors, troublemakers, turn coats, not to be trusted and various other demeaning attitudes. So why do we only laud the physical courage and not the moral courage? Both are commendable and desirable, but both are not received in the same manner.

It has been taught time and time again, in seminars, training classes and basic academies across the land. Police officers have got to routinely, daily, regularly, all the time, engage in conduct that is ethical and legal, regardless of the situation or individuals involved. Our approach must be to recognize, encourage and reward ethical behavior as unabashedly as we do the physical courage displayed under fire. At the same time, we, as administrators, citizens and leaders must discourage unethical and illegal conduct by meting out the sure, swift and certain discipline required for the conduct in question. The term, "Follow Me", is found in the U.S. Army and other such disciplines and is a rallying cry often heard, but while it is oft times only an audible cosmetic or balm, it is extremely accurate if practiced. The leadership, whether of law enforcement agencies, city or county government, the State or the Federal bureaucracies and any other organization, has got to be out front. These individuals must lead by actions and not just words. You can print rules and regulations, policies and procedures and other volumes until you numb the mind with words on paper, but if the leaders are not willing to "show" their written resolves by in person, daily and uncompromising conduct, the words, in and of themselves, will not get the job done. We should all pretend that we are from Missouri and say, "show me". The leaders that can cut it, will, and those who can't, will not. Those who will not, should be replaced and those who will, should be supported fully.

Characters shine only when the spotlight is on them. Character shines eternal, even in the darkness of turmoil and tumult.

The Author

CHAPTER TWELVE

WHERE IS HE?

Many people are not what they pretend to represent. What you see and hear, is not always what you get, or even what you want. Unfortunately, for all of us, for what used to be our way of life, for what used to be the bastion of justice, right and freedom, the ultimate goal for far too many, is greed. A greed of unlimited gluttony in personal ego, power, money, sex, influence, or whatever may be the desire of any particular individual.

In many ways of thinking I am an old fashioned man, from the "old school", who believes in patriotism, the flag, the Constitution, in doing ones duty, in honor and other similarly "outdated" beliefs. Honesty is something you either are or are not. It is like being pregnant, you either are or are not. There is no such thing as being a little bit pregnant, or honest. There are those, even some of my closest friends, who make light of my unwillingness to bend to the mighty wind of temptation and slovenliness. I have been referred to as "too honest for my own good" and I understand the context within which that statement was made, but, again, where does one draw the line. How far is one willing to go before you say enough. For me, I don't take even the first step in those directions. Is there any technique or method to guarantee that any police officer or public official will not become involved in corruption? NO!

Cops are no different from anyone else, in all respects, except, they voluntarily accepted a duty, took on a heavy responsibility, assumed a mantle of trust and swore to an oath of fidelity, honor and respect. In doing so, they set themselves apart.

Look at recent history. From Bethel to Brownsville, from Bangor to Beeville, from Los Angles to New York, from Seattle to Miami, and all points in between, corruption of public officials is present and on the rise. The work ethic has declined. The morale fiber has become threadbare. Quality leadership has become more of a topic of discussion than a fact of everyday life. Honor is in the eye of the beholder as it relates to the instant point in time or to a specific issue. We have become more socialistic, politically correct and expedient, increasingly hyphenated, sectionalistic, money oriented, disrespectful of any authority above self, self-centered and self-indulgent.

Today, I am fifty-five years old, with thirty years of quality training and experience in law enforcement, investigations, intelligence, security and management. Today, I am unemployed, too old, over qualified, the wrong ethnicity, a non-member of the good old boy network and a man who has done it right, even with my mistakes. It makes you wonder why you should work hard, learn, become proficient in your profession and most of all, why you should be honest and adhere to your duty.

The bottom line has been, is now, and will continue to be, that corruption exists in the police profession, politics, engineering, medical, attorney, labor, clerical, judicial, legislative and every other form of endeavor. ALL OF THEM?!!!! In my chosen profession, far too many officers/personnel violate the laws of the land. I was once ask, after leaving Donna, "did you learn anything?" The friend, one of those who has expressed the opinion that I should be more pliable, was aiming that comment at that subject. I told him, yes I did. He ask me, what the lesson was. Knowing he would bust at the answer, I replied, doing right doesn't count for squat, but I don't know how to do it any other way. Yep, I knew his response, as he shook his head, shook my hand and stated, I did not have to ask to know the answer. There are those who respect me, as he does, even though he plows the fields of greater reality and expediency. Financially, I am ruined. Assuming the care of my parents has not made things any better and there is always another crisis around the corner, but my wife, God love her, and I are determined to overcome and rebuild. Somewhere out there, is an entity or an individual who wants a slightly balding, paunchy old man who won't succumb to temptation, is loyal, and knows how to get the job done. Somewhere?

Pulling out of the roadside park, I again looked back at the twisted and seemingly deformed pin oak tree. I was looking at the throw back in time, the lizard. The Chameleon, a simplistic, yet intricate species, can and cannot be seen. Instinctively, I knew the Chameleon, a master at changing the image presented, was on that tree, like the corruption in every profession of society, but like me trying to observe the Chameleon, you cannot always see what you are looking at.

Postscript

It is March 24, 2001 and I am sitting at my computer reviewing and editing the second draft of this book. I am looking for those tiny imperfections and attempting to apply some final application of genius to this work. Yet, my thought processes are continually interrupted by history, more aptly, very recent history. Two days ago came an event of long making that I can relate to, having been there and done that, and that I can sympathize with, with another Chief. The scourge of corruption marches on. Beginning at about six o'clock in the morning, eight San Antonio Police Officers, one Bexar County Deputy Sheriff, one Our Lady of the Lake University Investigator and two civilians were arrested by members of the San Antonio PD and the FBI on Conspiracy, Narcotics and other criminal violations. This culminated an investigation which commenced in 1997, yet, undoubtedly, did not nab all of those who could have been. Curiously, it is déjà vu, for just two days prior to this marked event, I received my commission as a Deputy Sheriff, with the Bexar County Sheriff's Department. It makes one think that he is being followed or does not have the ability to perceive another bad situation. Then I realized, to myself, that what I have been preaching is true, corruption is everywhere, so do your job, do it right, obey the law and the regulations and watch your back. Sounds simple? Actually, it is simple.

It is now May 5 and I am being slow in conducting the makeover of this work and getting it to the publisher. Yet, that may have been fortuitous as more information has come out that should be included in this work. Last week it was revealed that FBI agents in Boston had conspired to falsify evidence and thus falsify incriminate a man for mob activities. This innocent man was convicted and has spent the past thirty years in prison for a crime he did not commit. That is right, thirty years. He was put there by members of the vaunted FBI and no one in the FBI did a damn thing about it all this time. The United States Congress is holding hearings on the matter. One agent who was involved made a very telling attitude comment before that congressional committee. To a question the agent responded, "what do you want? Tears!" The arrogance was obvious. Thus, with this incident and others in the past month, the list grows longer and longer. Our nation should be deeply ashamed.

Remember the Chameleon